THE DOGMATIC AND MYSTICAL THEOLOGY
OF JOHN DONNE

DR. JOHN DONNE

From the original picture by Vandyck, as reproduced in
Alford's edition of the works of Donne.

THE DOGMATIC AND MYSTICAL THEOLOGY OF JOHN DONNE

BY

ITRAT HUSAIN, M.A., Ph.D. (Edinburgh)

Carnegie Research Scholar in English, Edinburgh University

WITH A PREFACE BY

SIR HERBERT J. C. GRIERSON

GREENWOOD PRESS, PUBLISHERS
WESTPORT, CONNECTICUT

Originally published in 1938
by the Society for Promoting Christian Knowledge, London
and The Macmillan Company, New York, for the Church
Historical Society

Reprinted from an original copy in the collections
of the University of Illinois Library

First Greenwood Reprinting 1970

Library of Congress Catalogue Card Number 76-109753

SBN 8371-4243-1

Printed in the United States of America

TO
THE MEMORY OF MY BROTHER,
DR. IBNI-HASAN, M.A., PH.D. (LONDON),
(1898—1935),
PROFESSOR OF INDIAN HISTORY, OSMANIA UNIVERSITY,
HYDERABAD (DECCAN)

CONTENTS

PREFACE

By Sir Herbert J. C. Grierson

Mr. Itrat Husain came here some years ago with the intention of carrying further a study of the English poetry of the seventeenth century which he had begun in India, and of preparing for the Ph.D. a thesis on the mystical strain in the religious poetry of Donne, Herbert, Vaughan, Traherne, etc. I confess to having felt some trepidation at the thought of the subject as rather outside my ken, and at the further thought of its being undertaken by an Indian. But Mr. Husain's intelligence and genuine interest in both poetry and mysticism attracted me, and I was fortunate in securing for him and his work the interest of Professor A. E. Taylor, competent to deal with the subject from the theological side as I was not. The study which Mr. Husain produced greatly interested me, and gained the approval of such qualified judges as Professor Taylor and Miss Evelyn Underhill.

It was in the course of his methodical study of the poets in question that, for his own guidance, Mr. Husain prepared an anthology or index of Donne's pronouncements on various dogmas, theological and ecclesiastical and distinctively Anglican. Moved by some rather sweeping statements made recently regarding the sincerity of Donne's conversion, and his orthodoxy as preacher, divine and poet, Mr. Husain (having gained a Carnegie Scholarship for further research) resolved to undertake a detailed examination of Donne's theological position. The result is contained in the present volume. Mr. Husain has asked me to write a short preface. My own interest has been mainly in Donne's poetry, and I do not feel myself qualified to pass any judgment on a study in systematic theology. The more systematic theology becomes the more I feel unable to follow its definitions and distinctions. I shall therefore confine myself to recording some thoughts evoked by a reading of this volume in proof.

The first is my feeling of surprise and respect that a study of Anglican theology should have been carried out so fully, intelligently and lucidly by an Indian. It has increased the respect that I have come, during the last twenty years, to feel for the better Indian students who have come to our university. To come to this country as undergraduates in British universities is not, I think, the best course for Indians. But among the more advanced students, who come to read for a higher degree, I have found several whom I have been glad to know both as students and as friends. My intercourse with them has been less in college classrooms than in the quiet of my own study. They have been of all kinds and from all parts of India. With one who came less to study than to see how things were done at the Scottish universities I formed a specially close intimacy. He is now the head of a great Christian college at Trichur. Of the younger men I have met none who left on those who came to know him a stronger impression of ability and industry than Mr. Husain.

My second impression, which I record with some diffidence, is that Mr. Husain has established his main contention, viz. that Donne was in all his explicit statements on dogmas and practice an orthodox Anglican, almost too completely. The feeling one gets is that of acquiescence rather than of passionate conviction attained after much doubt and uncertainty. Donne writes somewhat as an advocate who, having accepted his brief, is prepared to defend every article of the creed he has adopted. But this is probably not altogether just. Donne had to pass through a double conflict, intellectual and temperamental. And the first was the easier, to convince himself of the reasonableness of the *via media* of the Anglican position between the Church of Rome and the extremer Reformers. More difficult had been the conflict with a temperament which, though I think fundamentally religious, was also both worldly and sensual. The evidence of that conflict is obvious in all his religious writings, especially the *Divine Poems* and the *Devotions on Emergent Occasions,* but also in some of the most eloquent passages of his great sermons.

The third impression made on me is perhaps too personal a one to dwell on. It is the attraction for my own mind of the sobriety, the humanity, the quiet reasonableness which dictated the English quest for a *via media.* On the cardinal, the burning doctrines of the day, Predestination, the Atonement, Free Will, the Sacraments, the reasonable compromise which the Church Divines sought for appeals to one who a little dreads too high flights. "When asked what constituted wisdom, Confucius replied : To cultivate earnestly our duty to our neighbour, and to reverence spiritual beings while always maintaining a due reserve may be called wisdom." "A due reserve" in attempting to define difficult doctrines, and in prescribing religious cults and duties, is what it seems to me is the attraction of the Anglican Church.

But what thus attracts some minds is also, I suppose, the weakness of the Church, and provokes the contempt of fuller blooded ecclesiastical bodies. She wants the fanatical drive which makes a crusading Church. When a wave of passion agitates her calm breast then she tends to move off towards the Left or towards the Right—towards Calvinism and a prophetic rather than sacramental conception of the ministry, in the Methodist and Evangelical movement; or to the Right, a Catholic revival, a revived emphasis on the Sacramental as the centre of Christian worship, the conception of the ministry not as preachers, teachers, exhorters but as the instruments of a great miracle and the trustees of authority to bind and to loose. The great divines and poets of the seventeenth century understood how to combine moderation and humility in definition and dogma with a passionate devotion to the central Person of Christian worship, and it is this which Mr. Husain has divined in his study of Anglican theology and mysticism. The fundamentals of Christian virtue are characteristically stated by George Herbert :

> " Mark you the floore? that square and speckled stone,
> Which looks so firm and strong,
>   Is *Patience:*
> And the other black and grave, wherwith each one
> Is checker'd all along,
>   *Humilitie:*
> The gentle rising which on either hand
> Leads to the Quire above,
>   Is *Confidence:*
> But the sweet cement, which in one sure band
> Ties the whole frame is *Love*
>   And *Charitie.*"

H. J. C. GRIERSON.

INTRODUCTION

THE idea of this study of John Donne's dogmatic and mystical theology arose out of my thesis for the degree of Ph.D. in English, Edinburgh University—*The Mystical Element in the Religious Poetry of the Seventeenth Century.* In order to study in detail the scholastic and mystical elements in Donne's thought I had prepared an exhaustive anthology of his Sermons illustrative of his dogmatic and mystical theology. I was struck by Donne's sincere defence of the Anglican doctrine and ritual, and decided to make a detailed and systematic study of his theology.

The *first* chapter deals with Donne's defence of the Anglican Church against the Puritans and the Papists alike; I have tried to show that his defence of the Anglican Church was as sincere as that of other contemporary divines, like Hooker and Bishop Andrewes, and I have given, where it was possible, parallel quotations to show their unanimity.

The *second* chapter deals with Donne as a theologian, his views on the creeds, the ritual, and the Sacraments of the Altar, with the Anglican view about the Eucharistic Presence and Sacrifice, with the Sacraments of Baptism and Confirmation, the number of Sacraments, the invocation of Saints, and prayer for the dead and other religious practices.

The *third* chapter is a detailed study of Donne's treatment of revealed theology which consists of :

(1) The doctrine of God.
(2) The Holy Trinity.
(3) Creation.
(4) Christology.
(5) The Incarnation and Pre-existence of Christ.
(6) The Resurrection.
(7) The Ascension.
(8) Angels.

The *fourth* chapter is a brief account of Donne's conception of the Fall and Sin, and I have pointed out how far he agreed with the Augustinian doctrine of the Fall, and the Thomist conception of sin.

The *fifth* chapter deals with soteriology (i.e. the Atonement,

Justification and Predestination). I have also discussed Donne's attitude towards Calvinism and his repudiation of the doctrine of Predestination.

The *sixth* chapter briefly describes Donne's views on *Eschatology,* i.e. Immortality, Heaven, Hell and Purgatory.

Thus these six chapters cover the whole field of dogmatic theology in a systematic way, a method which is usually employed by theologians in the division and treatment of their subject matter.

The *seventh* chapter is a study of Donne's mystical theology, i.e. of the various forms of prayer, conversion, repentance, purification, illumination and union. Though Donne shows a very wide acquaintance with the medieval mystics and scholastic philosophers, there is little in his prose writings about the experimental side of mystical theology, which lays down precepts and rules for prayer and mortification, a good example of which is Fr. Augustine Baker's *Directions for the Prayer of Contemplation;* there was hardly any scope in his sermons for such a treatment. In this chapter I have described Donne's views about the various elements of mystical theology and have also briefly touched on his own personal experience.

Donne's mysticism is independent of philosophy; he is interested in the practical, religious and empirical side of mysticism, the attainment of personal holiness, Illumination, through the adoration of Christ, His Passion and Crucifixion. Though Donne was greatly influenced by S. Augustine, his treatment of mystical theology, like that of S. Bernard (whom he quotes frequently), is practical and oratorical. S. Bernard's great achievement, as Dean Inge says, was " To recall devout and loving contemplation to the Image of the crucified Christ," [1] and it was this aspect of mysticism in which Donne was also deeply interested.

It was not Donne's aim, like Hooker's, to make a comprehensive and systematic survey of the Anglican theology; his views on the various doctrines and ritual of the Church are dispersed through the whole body of his sermons, and I had to piece them together to present a systematic view of his theology. I have tried to avoid generalizations about Donne's views on the different controversial problems of the seven-

[1] *Christian Mysticism,* p. 140.

teenth century theology and have given evidence from his Sermons and other prose works in support of my statements. Donne was not an original theologian, his aim in his Sermons was the exposition, the elucidation, and the defence of the doctrines, dogmas and ritual of the Anglican Church, and he brought his immense learning, his high and noble conception of the Church of Christ, and his acute analytical mind to bear on his task, which he so successfully performed. Donne's position as an Anglican theologian, which I have discussed in the second and third chapters, has received scant attention from his modern critics, in spite of his great popularity in recent years.

In his treatment of mystical theology too, Donne does not show himself an original thinker; but in those passages where he deals with the adoration of Christ as the Redeemer, Saviour and Lover, he rises to great heights of mystical ardour and exaltation, and there are several autobiographical passages (which I have quoted in the Appendix) where he speaks of having received from Christ " a modest assurance " of his own salvation. When one thinks of Donne's great learning, of his passionate religious sincerity, of his acute and sensitive mind, one cannot help regretting that he did not devote himself to a systematic exposition of the Anglican theology in a great treatise.

This book is the first attempt which has so far been made to study in a systematic manner the dogmatic and mystical theology of John Donne, and if I have succeeded, in however small a measure, in establishing Donne's position as a faithful and sincere son of the Anglican Church, and as one of those who like Hooker, Parker and Andrewes, defended her against the attack of the Puritans and the Papists alike, I shall not have laboured in vain. I have retained in the main the seventeenth century spelling and punctuation of Donne's sermons.

No critic in this century has done more than Sir Herbert J. C. Grierson to perpetuate the fame of Donne and it has been a rare privilege for me to have worked under his able guidance. This book owes much to his valuable help and suggestions. I would also like to thank the Trustees of the Carnegie Trust, who awarded me a research scholarship to enable me to undertake this work.

CHAPTER I

JOHN DONNE AND THE ANGLICAN CHURCH

It is not necessary here to describe Donne's reputation as a great preacher and controversialist in the seventeenth century, for this has already been done by Mr. Pearsall Smith[1] and Mrs. E. M. Simpson,[2] but in spite of his significant revival in this century, he has received no recognition as an eminent Anglican divine and theologian, for it has been generally assumed that circumstances and the lack of court preferment forced him to become a priest, and that his love of the Anglican Church was not so sincere as that of George Herbert or Bishop Andrewes. In fact, Sir E. Gosse, commenting on the three unpublished sonnets,[3] said that they betrayed his leanings to " certain Romish doctrines "[4] and that " they seem to prove that even after the death of his wife and his subsequent conversion, he hankered after some tenets of the Roman faith, or at least that he still doubted as to his attitude with regard to them."

This is to bring a very serious charge of insincerity against the greatest Anglican preacher of his age whom Walton called a " second Austin," and whose art of preaching he compared to the ecstasy of S. Paul,[5] and whom another contemporary likened to S. Chrysostom.[6] Donne himself had a very high conception of the office of the preacher ; and we can hardly expect him to be defending and preaching the Anglican doctrines in the pulpit, while writing divine sonnets to express his personal doubts about them. Donne declared in one of his sermons :

[1] In his Introduction to *Selected Passages from Donne's Sermons.*
[2] In *A Study of the Prose Works of John Donne,* by E. M. Simpson (Oxford), 1924.
[3] He is referring to the three sonnets beginning with the lines :
    (a) " Show me, dear Christ, Thy spouse so bright and clear."
    (b) " Oh, to vex me, contraries meet in one."
    (c) " Since she whom I knew hath paid her last debt."
[4] *The Life and Letters of John Donne,* by E. Gosse, II, pp. 109, 110.
[5] Walton says of Donne's preaching " carrying some, as S. *Paul* was to Heaven in holy raptures, and enticing others by a sacred art and courtship to amend their lives."
[6]   " Where wee that heard him, to ourselves did faine
      Golden Chrysostome was alive again."   Elegy by R.B.

" Religious preaching is a grave exercise but not a sordid, not a barbarous, not a negligent . . . so the Holy Ghost hath spoken in these Instruments, whom he chose for the penning of the Scriptures, and so he would in those whom he sends for the preaching thereof. . . ." [7]

This doubt of Donne's orthodoxy as a theologian and the sincerity of his conversion to the Anglican faith is based on the fact that so far no attempt has been made to discriminate between Donne's defence of the Anglican Church as one of the Reformed Churches on the one hand, and his conception of the universal Catholic Church on the other; in fact we possess no detailed study either of Donne's conception of the Anglican Church or of his defence of it as a true Apostolic and Catholic Church. The reason is not far to seek; nearly all his theology and his eloquent and reasoned defence of the Anglican Church is scattered in his sermons, which in the three folio volumes issued by his son cover about 2,000 pages and do not make altogether interesting reading; but the matter is further complicated by the fact that Donne's sermons were not meant to expound a system of dogmatic theology or define the basis of the Anglican polity; he has himself defined the nature and scope of his sermons.

" . . . That's a difference between *Sermons* and *Lectures*, that a Sermon intends *Exhortation* principally and *Edification*, and a holy stirring of religious affections, and then matters of Doctrine and points of Divinity, occasionally, secondarily, as the words of the text may invite them; But *Lectures* intend principally *Doctrinal points*, and matter of *Divinity*, and matter of *Exhortation* but occasionally and as in a second place." [8]

Thus his sermons were primarily " aids " to devotion, and he considered the exposition of the theological doctrines or the defence of the Anglican Church as of secondary importance; and so in order to describe his conception of the Anglican Church in a comprehensive way I had to piece together various passages scattered throughout his sermons.

Donne also tried to avoid the discussion of controversial points in divinity in his sermons; he declared in his *Essays in Divinity* that :

[7] *XXVI Sermons,* 2.
[8] *L Sermons,* 1.

" Moral divinity becomes us all, but natural divinity and metaphysic divinity, almost all may spare. Almost all the ruptures in the Christian Church have been occasioned by such bold disputations *de modo*." [9]

He is never tired in his sermons of advocating peace within the Church, and the necessity of avoiding theological controversies on points and doctrines which are not essential to salvation. He declared in one of his sermons :

" Our chiefest joy, is, for the most part, our *own opinions* especially when they concur with other learned and good men too.   But then, *Jerusalem* is our love of the peace of the Church ; and in such things as do not violate foundations, let us prefer *Jerusalem* before our chiefest Joy, love of peace before our own opinions, though concurrent with others." [10]

And Donne makes a distinction between the opinion of the people, and the declared opinion of the Church :

" For, this is that, that hath misled many men that the common opinion in the Church is necessarily the opinion of the Church. It is not so, not so in the *Romane* Church : There the common opinion is, That the blessed *Virgin* Mary was conceived without originall sin : But cannot be said to be the opinion of that Church ; nor may it be safely concluded in any Church." [10]

Donne avoided controversy on " indifferent " things, disputation and wrangling about minute and subtle points in theology because he believed that these could never lead one to salvation.   There are certain mysteries of religion which cannot be revealed ; they transcend the meaning which can be expressed in words, and it is impious to contend about them.

" And besides, when I remember that it was God which hid Moses' body, and the Devil which laboured to reveal it, I use it thus, that there are some things which the Author of light hides from us, and the prince of darkness strives to show to us ; but with no other light than his fire brands of contention and curiosity." [11]

After briefly describing Donne's views about controversial

[9] *The Essays in Divinity*, edited by Dr. A. Jessopp, p. 219.
[10] *L Sermons*, 39.
[11] *Essays in Divinity*, p. 30.

divinity, we can now proceed to examine his views about the Anglican and other Churches.

Donne believed that the Reformation was necessarily due to the corruption in the Roman Church, and he assigned the success of the Reformation to the divine dispensation.

" When the fulnesse of time was come, and that Church which lay in the bowels of the putative Church, the specious Church, the Romane Church, that is, those souls which groaned and panted after a Reformation, were enabled by God to effect it; when the Iniquity of Babylon was come to that height. That whereas at first they took of Almes afterwards . . . Monkes bought and Lords sold, nay Monasteries bought, and the crowne sold . . . and so, at last came to say, That all the States of all Christian Princes are held of the Church, and really may be, and actually are forfeited to her, and may at her pleasure, be re-assumed by her. . . . Since upon all these provocations God was pleased to bring this Church, the Reformed Church, not onely to light, but to splendor, He hath preserved this Church from perplexities. If they say, we are perplexed with differences of opinions amongst ourselves, let this satisfie them, that we do agree all, in all fundamentall things : And that in things much nearer the foundation than those in which our differences lie, they differ amongst themselves, with more acrimony and bitternesse, than we doe." [12]

He has compared the Reformed Churches to the Primitive Church in this that they both suffered persecution and, with the grace of God, emerged triumphant.

" Thou art my hiding place sayes the Primitive Church, and so may the Reformed Church say too. For when the Roman Church had made this *Latibulum,* this hiding place, this refuge from Persecution, Ermitages, and Monasteries, to be the most conspicuous, the most glorious, the most eminent, the richest, and most abundant places of the World . . . may the Reformed Church say, the Lord was their hiding place, that mourned for this, when they could not helpe, and at all times, and by all meanes that God attended them, endeavoured to advance a Reformation. And though God exposed them as a wood to be felled to a slaughter of twenty, of forty, of sixty thousand in a day,

---

[12] *LXXX Sermons,* 60.

yet *Ille absconsio,* He hath beene our hiding place, He hath kept the roote alive all the way; And though it hath been with a cloud, yet He hath covered us. . . ." [13]
He once told his audience not to be dejected or disappointed at the dissensions among the Reformed Churches, for it was neither Luther nor Calvin that founded the Reformed Church but God Himself, and He would take care of what He had slowly created in so many years.

". . . deject not thyself with ominous presages, and prophetical melancholy, thy God will overthrow this Religion, and destroy this work which his right hand hath been a hundred years in repairing, and scatter his corn which his right hand hath been a hundred years in purifying. Come not to say, It was but the passion and animosity of *Luther,* It was but the ambition and singularity of *Calvin* that induc'd this Religion, and now that this is spent, the Religion melts like snow. Take no such thought, be not afraid that the truth of God shall or can perish." [14]
Donne maintained that the Anglican Church was the true Apostolic Church and that if it did not believe in certain Roman doctrines, it was none the less a true Catholic Church; and while the Roman Catholics charged the Anglicans with a defective Church, they charged the Roman Catholics with a superfluous religion, in which things not necessary to salvation had been affirmed as doctrines essential for salvation.

" When the Romane Church charges us, not that all is not truth, which we teach, but that we do not teach all the truth, and we charge them, not that they do not teach all the truth; but that all is not truth that they teach, so that they charge us with a defective, we them with a superfluous religion, our case is the safer, because all that we affirm, is by confession of all parts true, but that which they have added, requires proofe, and the proofe lies on their side; and it rests yet unproved." [15]
In another sermon he declared that while the Anglican Church withholds nothing " that is necessary to salvation," in

---

[13] *Ibid.* See also *L Sermons,* 25, where he again compares the Reformed Churches to the Primitive Church.
[14] *XXVI Sermons,* 23. For other passages on the Reformed Churches see *L Sermons,* 32; *LXXX Sermons,* 13; *LXXX Sermons,* 72; and *L Sermons,* 25.
[15] *LXXX Sermons,* 29.

the Roman Church, "the Additionall things exceed the Fundamentall; the Occasionall, the Originall; the Collaterall, the Direct; And the Traditions of men, the Commandments of God." [16]   Donne was referring here to the additions which had been made in the Roman Creed in the Council of Trent, which made the reconciliation between the Roman and Protestant Churches impossible.   Elsewhere he said :

"Truly I had rather put my salvation upon some of those ancient creeds, which want some of the Articles of our Creed (as the *Nicene* Creed doth, and so doth *Athanasius*) than upon the *Trent* Creed, that hath as many more Articles as our hath." [17]

He once advised his audience not to follow the Roman Catholics in their "severity and cruelty" for they had applied

"all the capital and bloody penalties of the Imperial Laws (made against *Arrians, Manicheans,* Pelagians, and Nestorians, Hereticks in the fundamentall points of Religion, and with which Christ could not ensist) to every man that denys any collateral and sub-divided Tradition of theirs." [18]

Donne held that the refusal of the Roman Church to differentiate between the "fundamental" and "indifferent" points in religion was their greatest error, for according to the Roman Catholic Church "if a man conceive any doubt of the dream of Purgatory, of the validity of indulgence, of the Latitude of a work of Supererogation, he is as deep in the fagot here, and shall be as deep in Hell hereafter, as if he denyed the Trinity, or the Incarnation and Passion of Christ Jesus." [18]   Donne was also against the Roman Catholic conception of the Canon Law, which had an authority equal to that of the Scriptures.

"But on the other hand, they stray too, and further, That they deliver more than the Scriptures doe, and make other Rules, and canons equall to Scriptures . . . so that these men have put the salvation of the world upon another

---

[16] *LXXX Sermons,* 79.

[17] *LXXX Sermons,* 29.   For other references on this point see *LXXX Sermons,* 60; *LXXX Sermons,* 63.   In this last named sermon, he says "We deny all their new additions so as that we affirme all the old foundations."   See *L Sermons,* 14 for Donne's views on the ancient creeds.

[18] See *XXVI Sermons,* 23.

Science, upon another profession; It is not the *Divine,* that is the Minister of Salvation, but the *Canonist.* I must not determine my belief in the *Apostles Creed,* nor in *Athanasius,* nor in that of the *Nicen* Fathers; not onely not the Scriptures, but not the Councels, nor Fathers must give the Materials, and Elements of my faith, but the *Canon Law;* for so they rule it."

And he further complains that even this Canon Law in the Roman Catholic Church is not constant, for it may be altered any time due to political or other considerations.

" Gratian that hath collected the sentences of Fathers and Councels, and digested them into heads of Divinity, he is no rule of our belief, because, say they, he is no part of the body of the Canon Law; But they that first compiled the *Decretals,* and the *Extravagants,* and they who have since compiled more Decretals, and more *Extravagants,* the *Clementins,* and the *Sextins,* and of late yeares the *septins,* with those of *John the 22;* these make up the body of the Canon Law, and these must be our Rule; what to believe. How long? Till they fall out with some State, with whom they are friends yet, or grown friends with some state, that they are fallen out with now; and then upon a new *Decretall,* a new *Extravagant,* I must contract anew or enlarge, or restraint my old belief." [19]

Donne not only defended the doctrinal position of the Anglican Church, he also held, as Lancelot Andrewes had done in *Responsio ad Apologiam Card. Bellarmini,* that the Anglican orders were as valid as the Roman Catholic. Donne says that when the Roman Catholic controversialists charge the Anglicans with having " no church, no sacrament, no priesthood, because none are sent, that is, none have a right calling," they were content to be tried by " their own canons and their own evidences " to prove the validity of the Anglican orders:

" If they require a necessity of lawfull Ministers to the constitution of a Church, we require it with as much earnestness as they . . . we professe with Saint Hierome, It is no Church that hath no priest. If they require, that this spirituall power be received from them, who have the same power in themselves, we professe it too . . . no man can

[19] *L Sermons,* 27.

confer other power upon another, than he hath himself. If they require *Imposition of hands,* in conferring orders, we joyn hands with them." [20]

He thus maintains that the Anglican Church, like the Roman Church, had an " orderly derivation of power from one to another " ever since she became such a Church.

In another sermon he declared that the Anglican Church accepted all that the ancient Fathers and Creeds had taught, and if the Roman Catholics " thinke to perplex us with the Fathers, we are ready to joyne that issue with them ; where the Fathers speak unanimously, dogmatically, in matters of faith, we are content to be tried by the Fathers. If they thinke to perplex us with Councels, we will goe as farre as they in the old ones. . . ." [21] He held that the Anglican Church was the true Catholic Church, that his religion was " the same, that Christ Jesus and his Apostles proposed at the beginning, the same that the generall Councels established after, the same that the blessed Fathers of those times unanimously and dogmatically delivered. . . ." [22]

Donne denied the claim of the Roman Church to be the only Apostolic Church, and there are some very interesting passages on this subject scattered in his sermons.

" Tertullian says well, that the whole Church of God is one household : he sayes every particular Church is *Ecclesia Apostolica quia soboles Apostolicarum,* An Apostolicall Church, if it be an offspring of the Apostolicall Churches : He does not say *quia Soboles Apostolicæ,* because that Church is the off-spring of the Apostolicall Church, as though there were but one such, must be the mother of all : for, sayes he, *omnes primæ & omnes Apostolicæ,* Every Church is a Supreme Church, . . . as long as they agree in the unity of that doctrine which the Apostles taught, and adhere to the supreme head of the whole Church, Christ Jesus." [23]

Donne argued that though all the Churches which derived

[20] *L Sermons,* 40. Hooker also maintained that " I may securely con-clude that there are at this day in the Church of England no other than the same degrees of ecclesiastical orders, namely, bishops, presbyters, and deacons, which had their beginning from Christ and His blessed Apostles." *Ecclesiastical Polity,* Book V, Ch. LXXVIII.

[21] *LXXX Sermons,* 60 ; also see *LXXX Sermons,* 55.

[22] *L Sermons,* 18.

[23] *LXXX Sermons,* 42.

their origin from an Apostolical Church were Apostolical Churches, none had any Apostolical jurisdiction, and thus the claim of the Bishop of Rome to be the successor of S. Peter as Apostle was false.

" The Apostleship, as it was the fruitfullest, so it was the barrenest vocation; they were to catch all the world; there is their fecundity, but the Apostles were to have no successors, as Apostles; there is their barrennesse, the Apostleship was not intended for a function to raise houses and families; the function ended in their persons; after the first, there were no more Apostles . . . so then if the present Bishop of Rome be S. Peter's successor, as Bishop of Rome, he hath Episcopall jurisdiction there; but he is not S. Peter's successor in his Apostleship and onely that Apostleship was a jurisdiction over all the world. But the Apostleship was an extraordinary office, instituted by Christ, for a certaine time, and to certaine purposes, and not to continue in ordinary use. As also the office of the Prophet was in the Old Testament an extraordinary office, and was not transferred then, nor does not remaine now in the ordinary office of the Minister. . . ." [24]

Donne also maintained that as S. Peter's office as the Bishop of Rome was not mentioned in the Scriptures, it could not be made an article of faith.

" . . . then for matter of faith, we require Scriptures; and then we are confident, and justly confident, that though historically we do believe it, yet out of Scriptures (which is a necessary proofe in Articles of faith) they can never prove that S. Peter was Bishop of Rome or even at Rome." [25]

And thus a succession to the Bishopric of Rome could not be made an article of faith, and the Roman Church could not claim " an infallibility in that Church as that no successor of S. Peters can ever erre." [26] The Roman Church, therefore, had no jurisdiction over the English Church, which was as Catholic as the Roman Church.

" The Church loves the name of Catholique, and wherein she is harmonious, that is, those universall and fundamentall

[24] LXXX Sermons, 72.
[25] Ibid.
[26] Ibid.

doctrines which in all Christian ages, and in all Christian Churches, have beene agreed by all to be necessary to Salvation, and then thou art a true Catholique. Otherwise, that is, without relation to this Catholique and universall doctrine, to call a particular Church Catholique, (. . . that is, universall in dominion, but not in doctrine) is such a solecisme, as to speak of a white blacknesse, or a great littlenesse; A particular Church to be universall, implies such a contradiction." [27]

To Donne the Anglican Church was the true Catholic Church in the sense that all things "necessary to salvation" were taught there. Addressing his hearers he said :

"The Church is a Hill, and that is conspicuous naturally ; but the Church is such a Hill, as may be seene everywhere . . . trouble not thyselfe to know the formes and fashions of forraine particular Churches; neither of a Church in the Lake, nor a Church upon seven hills; but since God hath planted thee in a Church, where all things necessary for salvation are administered to thee, and where no erronious doctrine (even in the confession of our Adversaries) is affirmed and held, that is the Hill, and that is the Catholique Church." [28]

Donne advised the Anglicans not to search for a model Church in foreign countries.

"For, as *Moses* says, that the word of God is not beyond sea ; so the Church of God, is not so *beyond sea,* as that we must needs seek it *there,* either in a *painted Church* on one side, or in a *naked Church* on another; a Church in *Dropsie* overflowne with *ceremonies,* or a Church in *consumption,* for want of such ceremonies as the primitive Church found usefull and beneficiall for the advancing of the glory of God, and the devotion of the congregation." [29]

[27] *LXXX Sermons,* 71. In another sermon he said, "The true Church is that, where the word is truely preached and the Sacrament duly administered"; but only the Sacraments "instituted by Christ himself"; see *LXXX Sermons,* 6.
[28] *LXXX Sermons,* 76. Donne has also defined the Catholic faith in his Pseudo-Martyr: "That therefor is *Catholique* faith, which hath beene always and everywhere taught, and *Repentance* and Remission of sinners by the *Death* and *Resurrection of Christ* and such truths as the *Gospell* teaches are the *Doctrin* which coagulates and fathers the Church into a body and makes it Catholique," pp. 372, 373.
[29] *L Sermons,* 33.

He insisted that the great need of Christendom was to
cultivate moderation and avoid the multiplication of sects
among the Reformed Churches by agreeing on the fundamental doctrines of the Christian religion, leaving the use of
ritual and the form of the Church government to the
judgment of the individual Churches.   He says that the
Anglicans need not

" disparage, or draw in question any other of our *neighbour Churches,* who perchance, cannot derive, as we can,
their power, and their *Mission,* by the ways required, and
practised in the Roman Church, nor have had from the
beginning a continuance of Consecration by Bishops, and
such other Concurrences, as those *Canons* require, and as
our *Church* hath enjoyed.   They, no doubt, can justly
plead for themselves, that Ecclesiasticall positive laws admit
dispensation in cases of necessity;   They may justly
challenge a Dispensation, but we need none;   They did
what was lawful in a case of necessity, but Almighty God
preserved us from this necessity." [30]

Hooker also advanced similar arguments in defining his
attitude towards " certain Reformed Churches."

" Unto the complete form of Church Polity, much may
be requisite which the Scripture teacheth not, and much it
hath taught became unrequisite;   sometime because we
need not use it, sometime also because we cannot. In which
respect, for mine own part, I see that certain Reformed
Churches, the Scotch especially and French, have not that
which best agreeth with the sacred Scripture;   I mean the
government that is by Bishops . . . this their defect and
imperfection, I had rather lament in such a case than
exagitate, considering that men, oftentimes without any
fault of their own, may be driven to want that kind of
Polity or regiment which is best." [31]

Donne urged that the Christians should try to maintain
their unity in fundamental doctrines which could be proved
necessary for salvation on the authority of the Holy Scriptures,
and cease all controversies about non-essential, and " indifferent " things.

[30] *L Sermons,* 40.
[31] *Eccl. Pol.,* Book III, Ch. XI.

" . . . but that all should be believ'd, which is in any
of them, all which is sum'd up in the Apostles Creed. Now,
the reason expressed in that Article of our Church, why all
this is to be believ'd is, Because all this may be prov'd by
most certaine warrants of holy Scriptures." [32]
He calls the Church a pillar, because " For strength it is a
Pillar, and a Pillar for firmnesse and fixation," [33] but the glory
and brightness of the pillar is not the same in all ages, nor is
it a pillar fixed only to Rome.

" But yet the Church is neither an equall Pillar, alwaies
fire, but sometimes Cloud too; The Church is more
and less visible, sometimes in splendour, sometimes in
an eclipse; neither is it so a fixt pillar, as that it is not in
divers places. The Church is not so fixed to Rome, as that
it is not communicated to other Nations, nor so limited in
itselfe, as that it may not admit changes, in those things that
appertain to order and Discipline." [34]
Thus the Church is a pillar " Fixed, for fundamental things,
yet a moveable pillar, for things indifferent and arbitrary." [33]

Donne's ideal was not a self-sufficient national Church like
that of Calvin or Luther, but a super-national and universal
Catholic Church, agreeing as far as fundamental doctrines
were concerned, while free to adopt and modify their own
system of Church government and public worship. It was
only on this basis he thought that unity among the different
Churches of Christ could be maintained (but after the Council
of Trent, all hopes of reconciliation between the Reformed
and Roman Catholic Churches were lost) and, as we have
shown, his bitterest complaint against Rome was that it had
made " indifferent " things obligatory to men's conscience
even at the pain of heresy.[35]   He held that the question of

---

[32] *L Sermons,* 14.
[33] *LXXX Sermons,* 61.
[34] *Ibid.*
[35] He said about the Roman Church, " . . . it grows to be damnation
to-day, to believe so as a man might have believed yesterday and have
been saved, when they will afford no salvation, but in that Church which
is discernible by certain and inseparable marks, which our Countryman
Saunders makes to be six and *Mich. Medina* extends to eleven, and
Bellarmine declares to be fifteen, and *Bodius* stretches to a hundred,
when they make everything heresy . . . follow them not, do not imitate
them; be content to judge more charitably of them." *XXVI Sermons,*
23.

ceremony need not divide the Reformed Church into con-
tending factions, these could be retained or dispensed with
according to the need and will of the different Churches.[36]

" There are outward things, ceremoniall things, in the
worship of God, that are temporary, and they did serve
God that brought them in, and they doe serve God also,
that have driven them out of the Church, because their
undeniable abuse had clog'd them with an impossibility of
being restor'd to that good use, which they were at first
ordained for; . . . For all this separation, Christ Jesus is
amongst us all, and in his time, will break down this wall
too, these differences amongst Christians, and make us all
glad of that name, the name of Christians, without affecting in ourselves, or inflicting upon others, other names of
envy, and subdivision." [37]

He declared in another sermon that " cleaving always
intirely, and inseparably to the fundamentall truths of our own
religion, as farre as it is possible we should live peaceably with
all men." [38]   Donne's liberal views on religious toleration were
based on his belief that salvation could be achieved through
all those Christian Churches which believed in fundamental
doctrines.   He wrote in a letter to Sir Henry Goodyer
(1609):

" You know I never fettered nor imprisoned the word
Religion; not straightening it friarly, *ad Religiones factitios*
(as the Romans call well their orders of Religion), nor
immuring it in a Rome or a Wittenberg or a Geneva; they
are all virtual beams of one sun, and wheresoever they find
clay hearts, they harden them and moulder them into dust;
and they entender and mollify waxen.   They are not so
contrary as the North and South Poles, and that [?] they
are co-natural pieces of one circle.   Religion is Christianity,
which being too spiritual to be seen by us, doth therefore

<hr/>

[36] Hooker also said that the disputes " which have lastly sprung up
from complements, rites and ceremonies of Church actions, are in truth
for the greatest part, such silly things, that very easiness doth make them
hard to be disputed of in serious manner."   (Epistle Dedicatory to the
Laws of *Ecclesiastical Polity*.)

[37] *L Sermons*, 21.

[38] *L Sermons*, 18.   For other passages on this subject see *LXXX
Sermons*, 49; *L Sermons*, 21.

take an apparent body of good life and works, so salvation requires an honest Christian." [39]

Donne therefore preached the need of moderation towards both the Papists and the Puritans. In a remarkable passage he refers to those people who believe " that there is nothing done, if all bee not done; that no abuses are corrected, if all bee not removed; that there's an end of all Protestants, if any Papists bee left in the world." [40]   In a similar manner he advised his hearers to be more charitable towards the Calvinists; he held that the zeal which is directed to God but shows no charity towards men will not be acceptable to God.

" *Zeal* is directed upon God, and charity upon our brethren; but God will not be seen, but by that spectacle; nor accept anything for an act of Zeal to himself, that violates charity towards our brethren by the way. Neither should we call any man *Lutheran* or *Calvinist,* or by any other name, ignominiously, but for such things, as had been condemned in *Luther* or *Calvin,* and condemned by such, as are competent judges between them and us." [41]

Donne was also against condemning heretics to death.[42] But in spite of his realization of the need of unity among the Christian Churches, Donne is against any compromise on fundamental principles and doctrines. He says that Christ is the " God of Love, and peace, and unity," [43] and so one should try to assume a conciliatory attitude towards the other Christian Churches. He calls the " indifferent " things in religion silver, or sweat, while fundamental doctrines are gold and blood.

" If our Adversaries would be bought in with our silver, with our sweat, we should not be difficult in meeting them half way, in things, in their nature, *indifferent*. But if we

---

[39] E. Gosse, *Life and Letters of John Donne,* Vol. I, p. 226. In another letter to Sir Henry Goodyer (1615) Donne said, " I will not, nor need you to, compare the religions. The channels of God's mercies run through both fields; and they are sister teats of His graces. . . ." Gosse, Vol. II, p. 78.

[40] *L Sermons,* 18.

[41] *L Sermons,* 21.

[42] He said that we should follow the advice of S. Augustine in this matter: " Take not away the subject of that error, (the perverseness of the man) so, as that thou take away the subject of repentance, the man himselfe; If thou require fruit, leave a tree; If thou wouldst have him repent, take not away his life, sayes he." *LXXX Sermons,* 36.

[43] *L Sermons,* 41.

must pay our Gold, our *Blood,* our *fundamentall* points of Religion, for their friendship, A Fortune, a Liberty, a Wife, a Childe, a Father, a Friend, a Master, a Neighbour, a Benefactor, a Church, a World, is not worth a dramme of this gold, a drop of this Blood." [44]
In a letter to Sir Henry Goodyer (1615) he wrote that toleration in religion should not create the impression of weakness or indifference in matters of faith in others.

" But I am angry that any should think you had in your religion peccant humours, defective or abundant . . . yet let me be bold to fear, that the sound true opinion, that in all Christian professions there is way to salvation (which I think you think), may have been so incommodiously or intempestively sometimes uttered by you : or else your having friends equally near you of all the impressions of religion, may have testified such an indifferency, as hath occasioned some to further such inclinations as they have mistaken to be in you.

" This I have feared, because heretofore the inobedient Puritans, and now the over-obedient Papists, attempt you." [45]
Donne is equally emphatic in his denunciation of all kinds of schisms or sects within the Church. His sense of the continuity of the tradition and the ultimate unity of all the Christian Churches was so strong that he could not tolerate heresy in any form.

" Sects are not bodies, they are but rotten boughs, gangrened limmes, fragmentary chips, blowne off by their own spirit of turbulency, fallen off by the waight of their own pride, or hewn off by the excommunications and censures of the Church. Sects are no bodies, for there is . . . nothing common amongst them, nothing that goes through them all ; all is singular, all is . . . my spirit, and thy spirit, my opinion and thy opinion, my God and thy God ; no such apprehension, no such worship of God, as the whole Church hath ever more acquainted withall and contented with." [46]
He believed that " Christ loves not singularity ; he called not

[44] *L Sermons,* 41.
[45] Gosse, Vol. II, p. 78.
[46] *LXXX Sermons,* 74.

one alone; He loves not Schisme neither between them whom he calls." [47]   He declared that one who tries to break " the peace of the Church, by his Schisme, the *old serpent* hath bitten, and poysoned him, and shall bite worse hereafter." [48]

Donne was against hasty and too frequent excommunications. He said :

" Certainly there is much tendernesse and deliberation to be used, before the Church doores be shut against any man. If I would not direct a prayer to God, to excommunicate any man from the triumphant Church (which were to damn him) I would not oyle the Key, I would not make the way slippery for excommunication in the Militant Church."

Donne has made a distinction between schism and heresy. He defines schism as a " departure from obedience " and heresy as a " wilful deflection from the way of faith," [48] and though he maintained that excommunications in the Anglican Church never issue but on wilful " disobedience to the Church," there was need of great caution and moderation for every excommunication may not be " sealed in Heaven." [49]

There are several passages in his sermons where he has emphasized the fact that the establishment of a visible Church was necessary for salvation. He called the Church " the face of God to us," [50] and in another sermon he declared that " the ordinary place for Illumination in the Knowledge of God, is the Church." [51]   He said that we only " see " God in Nature, but we can " know " God only in His Church.

" By the light of Nature, in the Theatre of the World by the medium of creatures, we see God, but to know God, by believing, not only Him, but in Him, is only in the Academy of the Church, only through the Medium of the ordinances there, and only by the light of faith." [52]

[47] *LXXX Sermons,* 71.
[48] *Essays in Divinity,* p. 129. Donne held that heresy may sever one from the Church but may not wholly sever from God, while Hooker thought that " Both heresy and many other crimes which wholly sever from God do sever from the Church of God in part only."   *Ecc. Pol.,* Bk. V.
[49] *LXXX Sermons,* 66.
[50] *LXXX Sermons,* 29.
[51] *LXXX Sermons,* 23.
[52] *Ibid.*

He held that obedience to the Church was necessary for salvation.

"Hearken to the voyce of God, in the Church . . . so let no man presume a better state in the Triumphant Church, than he holds in the Militant, or hope for *Communion* there, that despises *excommunication* here." [53]

Donne believed that though some men may have a vision of God in this life, it is only a fleeting glimpse, for "he comes and he knocks, and he enters, and he stayes, and he sups and yet for their unworthenesse goes away again," [54] but He is always with His Church.

"Hee keeps us not in fear of Resumption; of ever taking himself from the Church again; nay he hath left himself no power of Revocation! I am *with you,* says he, to the end of the world." [54]

Donne declared that there was no remission of sin but through the ordinances and articles of the Church, though this remission has to be manifested in the amendment of life and the peace of the individual conscience.

"There is also a Remission; a Remission of sins. It is an Article of Faith, therefore believe it. Believe it originally and meritoriously in Christ; and believe it instrumentally and ministerially in the power, constituted by Christ, in the Church. . . . Hast thou sought thy Remission at the Church? . . . In which ordinances, there is an Infallibility of Remission, upon true repentances, and in a contempt or neglect of which ordinances, all Repentance is illusory, and all Remission but imaginary." [55]

He also demanded sincere obedience to the discipline of the Church.

"Come to the house of God, his Church; Joyne with the Congregation of the Saints; Love the body, and love the garments too; that is, the order, the Discipline, the Decency, the unity of the Church." [56]

He thought that those who relied on their own private prayers and devotions at home were neglecting the ordinances of God.

"So if every man think to provide himselfe *Divinity* enough at *home,* for himselfe and his family, and out of

[53] *L Sermons,* 33.
[54] *L Sermons.*
[55] *LXXX Sermons,* 28. Also see *L Sermons,* 17.
[56] *LXXX Sermons,* 51.

C

Laziness and singularity or State, or disaffection to the preacher, leave the *Church* unfrequented, he frustrates the ordinance of God, which is, that his sheep should come to his pastures, and take his grasse upon his ground, his instructions at his house at *Church*." [57]

He said that the Church was " the Spouse of Christ," [58] and the marriage of Christ to His Church was eternal.

" Christ is immortall, as hee is *himselfe,* and immortall, as hee is the *head* of the Church; the Husband of that wife; for that wife, the Church is immortall too." [59]

Thus the establishment and maintenance of the visible Church as the repository of the spirit of Christ was of fundamental importance to him.[60]   Donne's famous sonnet beginning with the line:

" Show me, dear Christ, thy Spouse, so bright and clear "

(which Sir Edmund Gosse published in his *Life and Letters of John Donne*) has given rise to much speculation about Donne's conception of the Church; it has been taken as a proof of Donne's insincerity to the Anglican Church; some critics have pointed out that this sonnet clearly shows that Donne failed to find the true Church of Christ. L. I. Brevold says that Donne searched in vain all his life " for a Church to which he could give undivided, uncritical allegiance. . . . Thus this man of unusual intellectual passion and power, whose desire for truth was deep and imperative, saw it always eluding his grasp; always a seeker after truth, but pursuing it in vain, he suffered painful dejection and disillusionment." [61]   Sidney Dark commenting on this sonnet has said, " But the priest, not yet a Dean, is still a doubter.   He

[57] *L Sermons,* 24.

[58] *L Sermons,* 27.

[59] *L Sermons,* 45.   Also see *LXXX Sermons,* 29, and *LXXX Sermons,* 32.   Donne said that while Scriptures are " God's voyce," the Church was " his Eccho, a redoubling, a repeating of some syllables, and accents of the same voice " (*LXXX Sermons,* 17).   For obedience to the Church see *LXXX Sermons,* 51 and 57.   For remission of sin through the Church see *L Sermons,* 17 and 28.

[60] Hooker also said: " For preservation of Christianity there is not anything more needful, than that such as are of the visible Church have mutual fellowship and Society one with another."   *Ecc. Pol.,* Bk. III, Chap. I.

[61] L. I. Brevold, *Religious thought of Donne in Relation to Mediæval and Later Traditions,* p. 213.

cannot even decide which is the true Church." [62] However, a careful study of Donne's *Essays in Divinity* and his sermons would convince anyone of Donne's deep attachment to the Anglican Church and his obvious sincerity in defending it against the Papists and the Puritans alike. Donne believed in the essential unity of all Christian Churches, and the desire that the unhappy division and sub-divisions in the Church of Christ should be reconciled to a perfect unity in doctrine and worship never left him. He had declared in *Essays in Divinity* when he was about to become an Anglican priest,

" and though to all my thanksgiving to God, I ever humbly acknowledge as one of his greatest mercies to me, that he gave me my pasture in this park, and my milk from the breast of this church, yet of a fervent and, I hope, not inordinate affection, even to such an unity, I do zealously wish, that the whole Catholic Church were reduced to such unity and agreement in the form and profession established in any of these Churches (though ours were principally to be wished) which have not by any additions destroyed the foundation and possibility in Christ Jesus; that their Church discharged of disputations, and misapprehensions, and this defensive war, might contemplate Christ clearly and uniformly." [63]

It is the same passionate desire for the unity of the Church that animates this sonnet and is not incompatible with his sincere belief in the Anglican doctrines. To him all the Christian Churches were the " virtual beams of one sun," and he thought it would advance the purpose and glory of Christ if all the different Christian Churches could again be united into one universal Catholic Church.

" Blessed be that God, who, as he is in all our foundations; And he in his time may bring our Adversaries to such a moderation as becomes them, who doe truly desire, that the Church may bee truly *Catholique,* one *flock,* in *one fold, under one shepherd, though not all of one colour,* of one practice in all outward and disciplinarian points."

Donne, in his sonnet, is perhaps comparing the divisions in the Christian Churches with the unity which Christ promised

[62] Sidney Dark, *Five Deans,* p. 93.
[63] *Essays in Divinity,* pp. 131, 132.

to His Bride (the Church) in Heaven as the Triumphant Church.

In an interesting passage in one of his sermons, which has so far not attracted the attention of his critics, Donne has enlarged on his conception of the " Spotless Spouse of Christ," which in this sonnet he calls " bright and clear."

Donne says that the aim of Christ was to make for " himself a glorious Church, not having spot or wrinkle," but the Church in this world is in a state of " pilgrimage and therefore here is no settling," and that it shall be only in Heaven that Christ shall have a Spotless Spouse.

" His end was, that *he might make it to himself a glorious Church, not having spot or wrinkle ;* but that end must be in the end of all ; here it can not be. Since as yet the whole Church sayes, *forgive us our trespasses,* the Church as yet is not without spots or wrinkles. The wrinkles are the Testimonies of our *age ;* that is, our sinne, derived from *Adam ;* and the spots are the sinnes which we contract ourselves, and of these spots and *wrinkles,* we cannot be delivered in this world . . . to settle such a glorious Church without spot or wrinkle, holy to himselfe, is reserved for the Triumphant time when she shall be in possession of that beauty which Christ foresaw in her, long before when he said, *Thou art all faire my love, and there is no spot in thee ;* and we that shall be the Children of the Mariage Chamber, shall be glad and rejoice, and give glory to him, because the Mariage of the Lambe is come, and his wife hath made herself ready." [64]

Thus when Donne asked,

" What ! is it she, which on the other shore
Goes richly painted ? or which rob'd and tore
Laments and mournes in Germany and here,"

he perhaps knew that these were idle questionings and that the vision of the True Church was reserved for the Elect in Heaven.

In another sermon Donne also referred to the same idea that all the ills of the Church cannot be mended here.

" They that make too much haste to mend all at once.
. . . They prevent Christ's Judgment, and rashly and sacri-

legiously they usurp the Angels office.   Christ hath reserved
the cleansing and removing of all scandals, all offences to
the last day;   the Angels of the Church, the Minister, the
Angels of the State, the Magistrate, cannot doe it;   nor the
Angels of heaven themselves till the day of Judgment." [65]
In spite of his sublime conception of the Universal Catholic
Church, he defended the *via media* of the Anglican Church
as the only sensible and reasonable solution which the
Reformed Churches could adopt.

" From extream to extream, from east to west, the
Angels themselves cannot come, but by passing the middle
way between;   from that extream impurity, in which Anti-
Christ had damped the Church, to that intemerate purity,
in which Christ had constituted his Church, the most
Angelicall Reformers cannot come. . . . It is the posture
reserved for heaven, to sit down, at the right hand
of God;   Here our consolation is, that God reaches
out his hand to the receiving of those who come
towards him;   And nearer to him, and to the institutions of
his Christ, can no Church, no not of the Reformation, be
said to have come than ours does." [66]

There are several passages in his sermons where Donne has
urged the necessity of a close union between the State and
Church;   he, like the other seventeenth century divines, also
believed in the divine right of the Kings;   to him " The Law
of the Prince is rooted in the power of God."   " The roote of
all is order, and the orderer of all is the King." [67]   His main
argument, however, was that it would be more conducive to
the preservation of order and discipline in the Church, as well
as the State, if the secular and spiritual " fraternity " were
joined together;   it was on this basis that he justified the
union of the State and the Church under the Crown.

" The Principall fraternity and brotherhood that God
respects, is spirituall;   Brethren in the profession of the same
true religion. . . . And that God loves that a naturall, a
secular, a civill fraternity, and a spirituall fraternity should
be joynd together; . . . God saw a better likelihood of

[65] *L Sermons,* 18.
[66] *L Sermons,* 27.
[67] *LXXX Sermons,* 69.

avoyding Schisme and dissention, when those whom he called to a new spirituall brotherhood in one Religion, were naturall brothers too; and tied in civill bands, as well as spirituall." [68]

---

[68] *LXXX Sermons,* 71.

CHAPTER II

JOHN DONNE THE THEOLOGIAN

No systematic and critical study of Donne's theology has so far been made except by Mrs. Simpson [1] in an interesting essay on the general outline of his theological beliefs, and in spite of his great popularity in this country, his position in the history of the Anglican Church remains undefined.[2] Though Henry Alford declared that after " obnoxious or trifling passages " have been struck out—he means the passages where Donne follows the Fathers—" there is left unimpaired a genuine body of orthodox divinty (in the best sense of the words) not to be found, perhaps, in any other English theologian," [3] and Dr. Jessopp had little doubt about Donne's orthodoxy as an Anglican divine once he had freed himself from " the thraldom of the Roman tyranny as formulated in the Tridentine decrees." [4] Donne is not recognized even to-day as one of the band of the seventeenth century divines, like Hooker and Bishop Andrewes, who tried to defend the Anglican Church and expounded its doctrines and ritual against the controversialists of other Churches.

Mr. T. S. Eliot has asserted that Donne had no settled belief in any philosophy. Speaking of his poetry, he declared :

" Donne was a learned student of philosophy. But his poetry is not that of a man who believes any philosophy. He enjoys his learning, and enjoys using a philosophical idea

[1] *A Study of the Prose Works of John Donne* by E. M. Simpson; Oxford, 1924.

Sidney Dark's Essay on Donne in *Five Deans* (1928) is very unsympathetic and uncritical and does not describe his theological views as the Dean at all.

[2] In the recent admirable anthology of the religious literature of the seventeenth century by Paul Elmer More and Frank Leslie Cross entitled *Anglicanism,* only one passage of Donne on " Hell " (p. 336) and one poem, " The Cross " (p. 776), have been included.

[3] *The Works of John Donne,* edited by Henry Alford, Vol. I, p. xxi.

[4] *John Donne* by Dr. A. Jessopp (1897), p. 136.

in poetry. His poetry expresses no settled belief in any-thing." [5]

He has expressed a similar opinion about Donne's thought in general which, according to him, is characterized by " a vast jumble of incoherent erudition on which he drew for purely poetic effects." [6]

Donne in his sermons, especially those on Christmas, Easter, Whitsuntide and the Holy Trinity, deals fully with the cardinal as well as controversial points of dogmatic theology. He defends the Anglican viewpoint against the Papists and the Puritans alike. He mainly takes his stand on the Apostles' and the Nicene Creeds and his exposition of the fundamental Christian doctrines is that of the orthodox Anglican divines, like Hooker, Andrewes and Laud, though he seems to have had little sympathy with the rigid ecclesiasticism of Laud. He said in one of his sermons about the Articles and Creeds of the Anglican Church :

"Amongst those *Articles,* in which our Church hath explained and declared her faith, this is the eighth Article, that the three Creeds (that of the Councell of *Nice,* that of *Athanasius,* and that which is commonly known by the name of the *Apostles* creed) ought thoroughly to be received, and embrac'd. The meaning of the Church is not, that onely that should be believ'd in which those *three creeds agree;* (for, The *Nicen Creed* mentions no Article after that of the *holy Ghost,* not The Catholique Church, not the communion of Saints, not the Resurrection of the flesh ; *Athanasius* his creed does mention the Resurrection, but not the Catholique Church, nor the communion of Saints) but that *all* should be believ'd which is in any of them, all which is summ'd up in the Apostles Creed. Now, the reason expressed in that Article of our Church, why all this is to be believed, is ; *Because all this may be prov'd by most certaine warrants of holy Scriptures."* [7]

That Donne was fond of preaching, and attached great

[5] " The Poetry of John Donne," *The Listener,* March 19, 1930. Donne, it is true, did not believe in one single system of philosophy as Dante did in the philosophy of S. Thomas Aquinas, but it cannot be said of his Divine Poems (even if we leave his Sermons aside) with their agony of purgation and passionate belief in the redemptive mission of Christ that they express " no settled belief in anything."

[6] *Selected Essays* by T. S. Eliot, p. 335.

[7] *L Sermons,* 14.

importance to it is evident from many passages in his sermons as well as his letters. He wrote to George Gerrad only two months before his death :

" I have been always more sorry, when I could not preach, than any could be, that they could not hear me. It hath been my desire (and God may be pleased to grant it me), that I might die in the Pulpit; if not that, yet that I might take my death in the Pulpit, that is, die the sooner by occasion of my former labours." [8]

He had a high sense of responsibilities of a preacher; he declared in one of his sermons :

" Religious preaching is a grave exercise but not a sordid, not a barbarous, not a negligent . . . so the Holy Ghost hath spoken in these Instruments, whom he chose for the penning of the Scriptures, and so he would in those whom he sends for the preaching thereof : he would put in them a care of delivering God's messages, with consideration, with meditation, and with preparation; and not barbarously, not suddenly, not occasionally, not extemporarily, which might derogate from the dignity of so great a service." [9]

He demanded from his audience the same dignity and reverence which he thought the preacher should himself possess; addressing his hearers once he said :

" When you come to hear us here, who are come from God, heare us with such an affection, as if we were going to God, as if you heard us upon your death-beds. The Pulpit is more than our death-bed, for we are bound to the same truth, and sincerity here, as if we were upon our death-bed, and then God's ordinance is more expresly executed here, than there." [10]

It is not surprising then that a man who considered sincere preaching as " inspired " with the spirit of the Holy Ghost should avoid the personal invective, be charitable to men of other faiths, and extend the promise of salvation to all Christians who believed in the fundamental doctrines of Christianity. In fact, Donne held that his sermons were

---

[8] Gosse, Vol. II, p. 268.
[9] *XXVI Sermons,* 2. Donne realized the need of frequent preaching; see *LXXX Sermons,* 57.
[10] *LXXX Sermons,* 47. For a detailed account of Donne's popularity as a great preacher, see Mr. L. P. Smith's Introduction to Donne's Sermons.

meant for " holy stirring of religious affections," [11] they were means of edification rather than lectures on divinity. Though Donne had made an extensive study of the " controverted divinity " of his age, he always tried to avoid it in his sermons, for he disagreed with the controversial methods of the contemporary divines. In a letter (1609) to Sir Henry Goodyer Donne, commenting on William Barlow's book, *An Answer to a Catholic Englishman,* he wrote :

" It hath refreshed, and given new justice to my ordinary complaint, that the divines of these times are become mere advocates, as though religion were a temporal inheritance ; they plead for it with all sophistications, and illusions, and forgeries : and herein are they likest advocates, that though they be fed by the way with dignities and other recompenses, yet that for which they plead is none of theirs. They write for religion without it." [12]

He expressed a similar opinion about the theological controversies in the interpretation of the Bible in his *Essays in Divinity.*

" . . . the spirit of God alone enlightens us best ; for many lights cast many shadows, and since controverted divinity became an occupation, the distortions and violencing of Scriptures by Christians themselves have wounded the Scriptures more than the old philosophy or Turcism."

This is why his discussion or exposition of dogmatic theology, such as the Christian Sacraments, or of the controversial doctrines, as of Predestination and Justification by faith, is based primarily on their ultimate bearing on the religious life of the soul, and secondarily on their relation to the contemporary theology.

DONNE AND THE SACRAMENTS

Donne attached the greatest importance to the proper administration and " holy " receiving of the Sacrament of the Altar. Its symbolism, its sacrificial aspect and its awful mystery, deeply interested him.

To him the significance of the Sacrament was that it was the vehicle for grace which the individual received in the act

[11] *L Sermons,* 1.
[12] Gosse, Vol. I, p. 221.

of receiving the Sacrament. He says that the Sacraments
" exhibit and convey grace; and grace is such a light, such
a torch, such a beacon, as where it is, it is easily seen." [13]
And though we recognize the grace when we feel it, we cannot
exactly describe how and when it enters.[13] Donne has
beautifully compared grace to the lustre in a precious stone,
and while we see the lustre, we cannot say how it entered the
stone.

> " As there is a lustre in a precious stone . . . so though
> we do not assign in the Sacrament, where, that is, in what
> circumstance or part of that holy action grace is, or when,
> or how it enters (for though the word of consecration alter
> the bread, not to another thing, but to another use; and
> though they leave it bread, yet they make it other bread,
> yet the enunciation of those words doth not infuse nor
> imprint this grace, which we speak of, into that bread),
> yet whosoever receives this Sacrament worthily sees
> evidently an entrance, and a growth of grace in himself." [13]

In the above passage he has expounded the Anglican view that
the bread is changed " not to another thing, but to another
use "; and though he emphasizes the necessity of the adoration of Christ in the Sacrament,[14] he maintains that there is
great difference between " an adoring of God in a devout
humiliation of the body in that action, and an adoring of the
bread, out of a false imagination that that bread is God " [15]

Like other Anglican divines Donne rejected the doctrine
of Transubstantiation.

> " There cannot be a deeper Atheisme, than to impute
> contradictions to God; neither doth any one thing so over-

[13] *XXVI Sermons*, 20.
[14] He says: " This Sacrament of the Body and Blood of our Saviour
Luther calls safely *venerabile & adorabile;* for certainly whatsoever that is which we see, that which we receive is to be adored for we
receive Christ " (*LXXX Sermons*, 68). It is exactly the same view which
Bishop Andrewes adopted about the " adoration of the Sacraments," that
the Anglican Church does not adore the Sacrament, but Christ in the
Sacrament. He says: " Now the King laid down that Christ is really
present in the Eucharist, and is really to be adored, that is, the reality
(rem) of the Sacrament, but not the Sacrament, that is, the ' earthly
part,' as Irenaeus says, the ' visible,' as Augustine says. We also, like
Ambrose, ' adore the flesh of Christ in the mysteries ' and yet not it but
Him who is worshipped on the altar " (*Responsio ad Apologiam
Cardinalis Bellarmini*). Quoted in *A History of the Doctrine of the
Holy Eucharist* by Darwell Stone, M.A., Vol. II, p. 265.
[15] *XXVI Sermons*, 20.

charge God with contradictions, as the transubstantiation of the Roman Church.   There must be a Body there, and yet no where; In no place, and yet in every place, where there is a consecration.   The Bread and the Wine must nourish the body, nay, the bread and the wine may poyson a body, and yet there is no bread, nor wine there. . . . And therefore *Luther* infers well, that since miracles are so easie and cheape, and obvious to them, as they have induced a miraculous transubstantiation, they might have done well to have procured one miracle more, a transaccidentation; that since the substance is changed the accidents might have been changed too; and since there is no bread, there might be no dimensions, no colour, no nourishing, no other qualities of bread neither; for, these remaining, there is rather an annihilation of God, in making him no God by being a contradictory God, than an annihilation of the Bread, by making that, which was formerly bread, God him selfe, by the way of Transubstantiation." [16]

Donne thus rejected the doctrine that there is any change in the " substance " of the bread, while in the same sermon he affirmed that the " elements " are changed, and that what was mere bread before has now become the Sacrament.

" That bread which thou seest after the consecration, is not the same bread, which was presented before; not that it is Transubstantiated to another Substance for it is bread still (which is the hereticall Riddle of the Roman Church, and Satan's sophistry, to dishonour miracles, by the assiduity and frequency, and multiplicity of them) but that it is severed and appropriated by God, in that ordinance to another use; It is other Bread, so, as a Judge is another man, upon the bench, than he is at home, in his owne house."

Bishop Andrewes also held that :   " But neither do we deny in this matter the preposition *trans;* and we allow that the elements are changed (transmutari).   But a change in substance we look for, and we find it nowhere. . . . At the coming of the Almighty power of the Word, the nature is changed so that what before was the mere element now becomes a divine Sacrament, the substance nevertheless

[16] *LXXX Sermons,* 4.

remaining what it was before." [17]   Like Andrewes and Hooker Donne also refused to define the manner of Christ's Presence in the Sacrament, for he held that this mystery was not revealed in the Scriptures for the guidance of His Church.

" But for the manner, how the Body and Blood of Christ is there, wait his leisure, if he have not yet manifested that to thee : Grieve not at that, wonder not at that, presse not for that; for hee hath not manifested that, not the way, not the manner of his presence in the Sacrament, to the Church." [18]

Andrewes also declared : " Christ said, ' This is my body.' He did not say, ' This is my body in this way ' . . . concerning the method of the presence, we define nothing rashly, and, I add, we do not anxiously inquire, any more than how the blood of Christ washes us in our Baptism, any more than how the human and divine natures are united in one Person in the Incarnation of Christ." [19]   Though Donne rejected Transubstantiation, he affirmed the real presence of Christ and thus repudiated the Zwinglian doctrine that the elements were only signs of the body and blood of Christ.

" Since Christ forbore not to say, This is my body, when he gave the sign of his body, why should we forbear to say of that bread, this is Christ's body, which is the Sacrament of his body ? " [20]

The Sacraments were not mere symbols or signs, but *actual* and effective instruments of divine grace. Hooker also held the same view.

" For we take not Baptism nor the Eucharist for bare *resemblances* or memorials of things absent, neither for *naked signs*, and testimonies assuring us of grace received before, but (as they are indeed and in Verity) for means effectual whereby God when we take the Sacraments

[17] *Works* (Anglo-Catholic Library), Vol. III, pp. 262, 265. W. Laud also rejected Transubstantiation. He said: " Transubstantiation . . . was never heard of in the Primitive Church, nor till the Council of Lateran, nor can it be proved out of Scripture ; and, taken properly, cannot stand with the grounds of Christian Religion " (*Works*, Anglo-Catholic Library, Vol. II, p. 306).
[18] *LXXX Sermons*, 4.
[19] *Works*, Vol. VIII, p. 13.
[20] *LXXX Sermons*, 4. Andrewes also declared, " We believe no less than you (Bellarmine) that the presence is real."

delivereth into our hands that grace available unto eternal life, which grace the Sacraments represent or signify." [21] Donne recognized the sacrificial aspect of the Eucharist in relation to the worthiness of the receiver on which he has laid great stress.

"Every man should come to that Altar, as holy as the Priest, for there he is a Priest. . . . Live in remembrance, that thou wast a Priest to-day (for no man hath received Christ, that hath not sacrificed himself)." [22]

To Donne the real significance of the Eucharist was that it could transform the life of the worthy receiver, for it was a means of the sacramental union with Christ. He calls the Incarnation the "naturall union," for Christ "hath taken our Nature," and Christ's union with His Church is the "mysticall union," but the Eucharist is the "sacramental union" with the body of Christ, for :

"when we receive the visible seales thereof worthily, we are so washed in his blood, as that we stand in the sight of his Father, as cleane, and innocent, as himselfe, both because he and we are thereby become one body and because the garment of his righteousness covers us all." [23]

Hooker took a similar view of the purpose of the Sacraments.

"Sacraments are the powerful instruments of God to eternal life. For as our natural life consisteth in the union of the body with the soul, so our life supernatural in the union of the soul with God. And forasmuch as there is no union of God with man without mean between both which is both, it seemeth requisite that we first consider how God is in Christ, then how Christ is in us, and how the Sacraments do serve to make us partakers of Christ." [24]

To George Herbert also the real merit of the Eucharist was that it washed away sins, gave "nourishment and strength" to the soul. It was the grace of Christ which could alone penetrate into the innermost parts of the human soul.

---

[21] *Ecc. Pol.*, Bk. V, Chap. I.
[22] *LXXX Sermons*, 4. He also equally insists on the worthiness and holiness of the Priest. He compares the "unworthy giver" to "Judas that pretended to be the Priest."
[23] *L Sermons*, 8.
[24] *Ecc. Pol.*, Bk. V.

" Onely thy grace, which with these elements comes,
Knoweth the ready way,
And hath the privie key,
Opening the souls most subtle rooms :
While those to spirits refin'd at doore attend
Despatches from their friend."

(The Holy Communion.)

Though Donne thought that the kneeling at the Sacrament was not " absolutely necessary " [25] and essential for salvation, yet out of respect for the Presence of Christ, the Communicant should kneel, for " he that feels Christ, in the receiving of the Sacrament, and will not bend his knee, would scarce bend his knee, if he saw him." [26]   Donne calls the sacraments of baptism and that of the Supper " permanent sacraments " instituted by Christ as " visible and sensible " [27] assistances to help our infirmity.   It is significant to note that Donne pointed out that the Word of God had a priority over the Sacrament, for " When Christ had undertaken that great work of the conversion of the world, by the Word, and Sacraments, to shew that the Word was at that time the more powerful means of those two." [27]   And he calls miracles " transitory and occasionall Sacraments," for they are also the " visible signes of invisible grace," [27] but they were only the signs and not like the Sacraments, the " seale of grace."

Donne attached great importance to Christian Baptism for it signified the birth of the individual soul into the Christian Church.   He believed that the decrees of God were exemplified in the Sacraments, and that one could not attain salvation without being duly baptized.

" As we cannot see the Essence of God, but must see him in his glasses, in his *Images,* in his *Creatures,* so we cannot see the decrees of God, but must see them in their *duplicates,* in their *Exemplification* in the *Sacraments* . . . yea if an Angel from heaven come downe and tell thee, that he saw thy name in the booke of life, if thou have not this Exemplification of the decree, this Seale, this

[25] *LXXX Sermons,* 12.
[26] *LXXX Sermons,* 68.
[27] *LXXX Sermons,* 11.

Sacrament, if thou beest not *baptized,* never delude thyself
with those imaginary assurances." [28]
Jeremy Taylor thought that Baptism was necessary for the
soul of the infants.

" Either the infants cannot go to Heaven any way that
we know of, or they must be baptized. To say they are
to be left to God is our excuse, and no answer. For when
God hath opened the door and calls that ' the entrance into
Heaven,' we do not leave them to God when we will not
carry them to him in the way which he hath described
and at the door which himself hath opened. We leave
them indeed, but it is but helpless and destitute." [29]
Donne, however, did not share the popular belief that the
souls of the unbaptized infants were damned, though he
emphasized the necessity of immediate baptism after birth.

" God can preserve the child without *Milke;* and he can
save the child without a Sacrament; but as that mother
that throwes out, and forsakes her child in the field or
wood is guilty before God of the Temporall murder of that
child, though the child die not, so are those parents of a
spirituall murder, if their children, by their fault die
unbaptised, though God preserve that child out of his
abundant, and miraculous mercy, from spirituall destruction." [30]
Donne refuted the argument of the Anabaptists that a child
should not be baptized till he is able to receive the other
Sacrament by pointing out that Christ Himself took the Sacrament of Baptism before He had instituted any other Sacrament.

" Christ took this Sacrament, his Baptisme, before he did
any other thing; and he tooke this three yeares before the
institution of the other Sacrament of his body and his blood.
So that the Anabaptists obtrude a false necessity upon us,
that we may not take the first Sacrament, Baptisme, till
we be capable of the other Sacrament too; for, first in
nature . . . we are borne before we are fed, and so in

---

[28] *L Sermons,* 7. Hooker did not commit himself to this view; he said
that when Christ Himself required baptism, " it is not for us that look
for salvation to sound and examine him whether unbaptized men may be
saved; but seriously to do that which is required and religiously to fear
the danger which may grow by the want thereof " (*Ecc. Polity,* Bk. V).
[29] See *The Great Exemplar,* Part I, Section IX.
[30] *L Sermons,* 7.

Religion, we are first borne into the Church (which is done by Baptisme) before we are ready for that other food, which is not indeed milk for babes, but solid meat for stronger digestions." [31]

Donne also defended the Anglican form of being baptized only in the name of Christ, as against the Roman Catholic form in which the Virgin Mary is also included.

" When therefore they teach in the *Romane Church,* that it is a good forme, *I baptise thee in the name of the Father, and Sonne, and Holy Ghost, and the Virgin Mary,* if he which baptises so, doe not meane in his intention, that the Virgin Mary is *equall* to the Trinity, but onely an *Assistant,* this is not onely an impertinence but an impious addition to that God, that needs no Assistant. And as in our baptisme, we take no other name necessarily, but the name of Christ; so in our Christian life, we accept no other distinction of *Jesuits* or *Franciscans,* but onely Christians; for we are baptized *into his name,* and the whole life of a regenerate man is a Baptisme." [32]

Donne also believed in confessing and openly acknowledging one's sins, which he called the " Sacrament of Confession." He points out that " publishing " of sin by " way of glory in that sin " is a great sin for it might lead others to commit the same sin, but " there is a publication of sin that both alleviates, nay annihilates my sin, and makes him that hates sin, Almighty God, love me the better for knowing me to be such a sinner than if I had not told him of it." [33]

Donne repudiated the Roman Catholic doctrine of the Sacrament of Confirmation. He says that in the Primitive Church the confirmation of Baptism did not imply the inadequacy of the Sacrament of Baptism, but that " it was a Confirmation of Christians, with an encrease of grace, when they came to such yeares, as they were naturally exposed to some tentations." [34] He further explains the Anglican conception of this Sacrament.

" Our Church acknowledges the true use of this Confirmation for, in the first Collect in the office of Confirmation, it confesses, that that child is already regenerated by

[31] *LXXX Sermons,* 43.
[32] *L Sermons,* 7.
[33] *LXXX Sermons,* 58.
[34] *LXXX Sermons,* 33.

water and the Holy Ghost, and prayes onely for further strength . . . For, he is but an interpretative, but a presumptive Christian, who, because he is so old ventures upon the Sacrament." [34]

It is not the age but the spiritual life of the Communicant that matters and therefore the Church enjoins "a precedent confirmation, where that is not, wee require yet a precedent Examination, before any bee admitted, at first, to the Sacrament."

Donne also rejected the Roman Catholic conception of marriage as a Sacrament. He agreed that the Roman Church has incorrectly translated those verses where they claim that marriage has been called a Sacrament.

"But for marriage amongst Christians, *Sacramentum hoc magnum est* (Eph. v. 32), saies the Apostle, *This is a great Secret, a great mystery.* Not that it is therefore a *Sacrament, as Baptisme,* and the *Lord's Supper* are *Sacraments.* For if they will make marriage such a Sacrament, because it is expressed there in that word, *magnum Sacramentum* (Rev. xvii. 5), they may come to give us eight Sacraments after their *seven;* They may translate that name which is upon the mother of Harlots, and abomination of the earth, *Sacrament,* if they will, for it is the same word, in that place of *Revelation,* which they translate Sacrament in the other place to the Ephesians; And in the next verse but one, they doe translate it so there; I will tell, saies the Angel, *Sacramentum mulieris,* the *Sacrament of Babylon.*"

Marriage to Donne was " magnum mysterium," a mysterious signification of the *union of the soule* with Christ " when both persones professe the Christian Religion, in *generall,*" but when both of them professe Christ in "one forme, in one Church" by this "significative union" "they are made *Idem spiritus cum Domino;* the same spirit with the Lord." [35]

Donne did not recognize the Sacraments as all sufficient vehicles of the divine grace, there were other degrees of grace which could only be acquired by living a holy life, which he calls "a confirmation" to the Sacrament. He beautifully compares the life of the Christian soul to Jacob's ladder and recognizes that it has to pass through several

[35] *L Sermons,* 1.

difficult stages, before it can achieve that degree of holiness, when it can behold God :

" Behold the life of a Christian is a Jacob's Ladder, and till we come up to God, still there are more steps to be made, more way to bee gone. Briefly, to the most learned, to him that knows most, to the most sanctified, to him that lives best, . . . there is a farther degree of knowledge, a farther degree of goodnesse, proposed to him, than he is yet attained unto." [36]

DONNE AND THE CEREMONIES IN THE CHURCH

Donne thought that as the purity of the individual conscience, and religious zeal were not enough and the community required the establishment of a visible Church, and outward discipline to direct its spiritual life, he also believed that the ceremonies were necessary for edification and for the devotional life within the Church in general.

" It is not enough for a man to believe aright, but he must apply himself to some church, to some outward form of worshipping God; It is not enough for a Church, to hold no error in *doctrine* but it must have *outward assistances* for the devotion of her children, and *outward decency* for the glory of her God." [37]

He held that the ceremonies should be retained as a means of edification for the " weaker sort of people," but should not be made an essential part of the Service of God.[38] He points out that the mistake of the Roman Church was that the ceremonies which were " significative " were made " effective."

" To those ceremonies, which were received as . . . helps to excite, and awaken devotion, was attributed an operation, and an effectual power, even to the ceremony itself; and they were not practised as they should, *significative,* but *effective;* not as things which should signifie to the people higher mysteries, but as things as powerfull, and effectual in themselves as the greatest Mysteries of all, the Sacraments themselves." [38]

[36] *LXXX Sermons,* 43.
[37] *L Sermons,* 41.
[38] *LXXX Sermons,* 8.

But Donne attached a great spiritual significance to the ritual of the Church.   In another sermon he said :

" He that undervalues outward things in the religious service of God, though he begin at ceremonial and ritual things, will come quickly to call Sacraments but outward things, and Sermons and Public Prayers but outward things in contempt. . . . Believe outward things apparel God; and since God was content to take a body, let us not leave him naked nor ragged."

He believed that the symbolic as well as the inward and spiritual content of the doctrine of the Church were inter-dependent.   He said in the same sermon that " He that cares not though the material Church fall, I am afraid is falling from the spiritual."   He thought that the Roman Church has abused the ritual of the Church by making it something more than symbolism.   Hooker also advanced a similar opinion about the proper use of the ceremonies.

" Those our ceremonies which they reckon most Popish . . . all are such as having served to good purpose, were afterwards converted unto the contrary.   And sith it is not so as much objected against us, that we retain together with the evil wherewith they have been infected in the Church of Rome, I would demand who they are whom we scandalize, by using harmless things unto that good end for which they were first instituted." [39]

Donne held that these ceremonies were not " the institutions of God immediately " but that they were " a kind of light earth, that hath *under it* good and usefull significations," but the Roman Church has made the ceremonies, like the traditions, as obligatory on man's conscience as the laws con-tained in the Scriptures.

" We deny not there are *Traditions,* nor that there must be *ceremonies,* but that matters of *faith* should depend on these, or be made of these, that we deny; and that they should be made equall to *Scriptures;* for with that especially doth Tertullian reproach the Heritiques, that being pressed with Scriptures, they fled to Traditions, as things equall or superior to the word of God." [40]

Donne recognized that the ceremonies and the use of Images

[39] *Ecc. Pol.,* Bk. IV.
[40] *L Sermons,* 24.

have been grossly abused in the Roman Church,[41] but he said
it was no argument, as the Puritans thought, for abolishing
them altogether.

" Woe to such advancers of Images, as would throw
down Christ, rather than his Image. But . . . woe to such
peremptory abhorrers of pictures and to such uncharitable
condemners of all those who admit any use of them, as had
rather throw down a Church, than let a Picture stand." [42]
Discussing the use of candles in the divine service, Donne
quotes Calvin as saying that because things good in their
institution may be depraved in their practice, the Church
should not deny the people all ceremonies for their edification
and as " assistance of their weaknesse." " Sayes he (Calvin)
. . . I think these kinds of helps to be very behoovefull for
them . . . all that I strive for, is but Moderation," and this
moderation in the use of ceremonies he explains as consisting
in that " these ceremonies may be few in number; That
they may be easie for observation; That they may be clearly
understood in their signification; we must not therefore be
hasty in condemning particular ceremonies: For, in so doing,
in this ceremony of lights, we may condemne the Primitive
Church, that did use them, and we condemne a great and
noble part of the reformed Church, which doth use them at
this day." [43] Though Donne might argue on a broad principle
that the ceremonies were not necessary for salvation, and that
those Churches which have rejected them altogether are still
the true Church of Christ, his heart was in the splendour and
outward glory of the Church.

" God is said in the Scriptures to apparell himself
gloriously *(God covers him with light as with a garment)* ;
And so of his Spouse the Church it is said (Her clothing is of
wrought gold, and her raiment of needle worke) and, as
though nothing in this world were good enough for her
wearing, she is said *to be clothed with the sun.*" [44]
Donne conceived the Kingdom of God as based on the glory
and majesty of the Church of God, where unanimity in

[41] He calls " their manifold, and scornfull, and ridiculous and
historicall *ceremonies* in their service," and the " dangerous poysons, the
direct Idolatries " as contrary to the Practice of the Primitive Church
(*L Sermons,* 24).
[42] *L Sermons,* 41.
[43] *LXXX Sermons,* 8.
[44] *LXXX Sermons,* 72.

fundamental doctrine, charity in non-essentials was the rule, where order, decency and outward splendour accompanied the inner purity of the devotional life of the Church.

" The Church of God requires also, besides unanimity in fundamentall Doctrines, an equanimity, and a mildnesse, and a Charity, in handling problematicall points, and also requires order, and comelinesse in the outward face, and habit thereof. And so we preach a Kingdome. . . . And we banish all spiritual felony or robbery, in despoyling the Church, either of Discipline, or of possessions, either of order, or of ornaments. *Be the King's daughter* all glorious within; yet all her glory is not within; For, *Her clothing is of wrought gold* . . . still may she glory in her internall glory, in the sincerity, and in the integrity of Doctrinall truths, and glory too in her outward comelinesse and beauty. So pray we, and so preach we the Kingdome of God." [45]

DONNE ON PRAYER TO THE SAINTS

Though Donne had a great reverence and love for the commemoration of the great Saints on their particular festival days (and he has preached several sermons on All Saints' Day, on the conversion of S. Paul, and the Candlemas Day), he did not believe in prayers to the Saints. He held that we should neither rely on the prayers of the Angels, whom he calls " ministeriall spirits," nor on those of the Saints. " Nor of Saints; Though they have a more personall and experimentall sense of our miseries than Angels have, we must not relie upon the prayers of Saints," [46] for a sincere and real prayer must be between God and Man alone. In another sermon Donne has compared the prayers to the Saints to the pagan practice of invoking and praying to their several deities which was condemned by Justin Martyr.[47] He asks:

" Why should I pray to *S. George* for victory, when I may go to the Lord of Hosts, Almighty God himselfe, . . .

---

[45] *LXXX Sermons*, 47.
[46] *LXXX Sermons*, 13.
[47] " It is a strange thing, sayes *Justin Martyr*, to pray *Esculapius*, or to *Apollo*, for health as Gods thereof . . . why should they not rather pray to their Masters, than to them? Why should *Apollo, Chiroes* Scholar, and not *Chiro, Apollo's* Master, be the god of physick? " (*LXXX Sermons*, 9).

or to another Saint for peace, when I may goe to the
Prince of peace Christ Jesus?   Why should I pray to
Saint *Nicolas* for a faire passage at sea, when he that
rebuked the storme is nearer me than S. *Nicolas?* " [48]
Donne even doubts whether some of these Saints ever
existed or all their legends were based on facts.

" I know not whether those Saints were ever upon earth
or no; our Adversaries will not say, that all their Legends
were really, historically true, but that many of them are
holy, but yet symbolicall inventions, to figure out not
what was truly done before, but what we should endeavour
to doe now.   I know my Redeemer liveth, and I know
where he is; and no man knowes, where he is not.   He is
our creditor, to him we must pray." [49]
Donne thought that the prayers for the dead were not
essential, but he would not condemn S. Augustine's prayer
for Monica.   " God forbid wee should condemne *Augustine*
or *Ambrose* of impiety in doing so, but God forbid wee should
make *Augustine* or *Ambrose* his example, our rule to doe so
still." [50]

DONNE'S CONCEPTION OF SALVATION

It is in Donne's conception of salvation that we discern
his breadth of vision and Christian charity which could not
be fettered or confined into the narrow sectarian bounds.   He
extended salvation not only to all the Christian Churches but
to those godly souls also who were not Christians.

" For though God have revealed no other way of
salvation *to us*, but by breeding us in his Church, yet we
must be so far from straitning salvation, to any *particular
Christian Church*, of any subdivided name, *Papist* or
Protestant, as that we may not straiten it to be the *whole
Christian Church*, as though God *could* not, in the largenesse of his power or *did* not, in the largenesse of his mercy,

---

[48] *Ibid.*
[49] *LXXX Sermons,* 9.   Donne seems to have believed in different
degrees of godliness attained by the Saints in Heaven; he did not think
that they all were blessed with the same measure of glory: " So for
those blessed souls which are collected into their eternall dwelling in
Heaven which have their immoveable possession, position at the right
hand of God, as one star differs from another in glory so do these Saints
which are in Heaven."
[50] *LXXX Sermons,* 5.

afford salvation to some, whom he never gathered into the Christian Church." [51]
He thought that all those who " professe the name of Christ Jesus aright " make up " but one body " [52] and Christ is the promise of eternal salvation to them all.

" My witnesse is in Heaven, my judge is in Heaven, my Redeemer is in Heaven, and in them, who are but one, I have not only a constant hope that I shall be there too, but an evident assurance, that I am there already, in his person." [53]

Donne makes salvation dependent on the degree of the knowledge of God, and this, in its fulness, he believes can only be attained in the Christian Church. If a man is a "morall man " and refers all his action to the " law of Nature in our hearts," this is for him the " Dawning of the day," a beginning of the knowledge of God, and if a man is a " godly man " and refers all to God, this is for him a " twilight," but he points out that the brightness of the noon, the fulness of knowledge can only be achieved through Christ.

" But the Meriodionall brightnesse, the glorious noon, and height, is to be a Christian, to pretend to no spirituall, no temporall blessing, but for, and by, and through, and in our Lord and Saviour Christ Jesus." [54]

Donne argued that the Christian knowledge of God was not simply an affirmation of the existence of God and His glory but it consisted in *a new revelation* of God.

" Knowest thou that there is a God, and that that God created the world? What great knowledge is this? The Jews know it too. . . . It is another Religion, another point of Faith, to know that God had a Son of eternal begetting and to have a world of late making. God therefore hath shin'd in no man's heart till he know the glory of God in the face of Jesus Christ, till he come to the manifestation of God in the Gospel. So that, that man comes short of this light, that believes in God, in a general, in an incomprehensible power, but not in Christ; and that man goes beyond this light, who will know more of God than is manifested in the Gospel, which is the face of Christ

[51] *L Sermons,* 25.
[52] *LXXX Sermons,* 10.
[53] *LXXX Sermons,* 13.
[54] *LXXX Sermons,* 19.

Jesus; the one comes not to the light, the other goes beyond, and both are in blindness." [55]
Though Donne believed that the people who do not profess Christ might be saved through the infinite mercy of God, the Christian Churches had no right to promise salvation to those who were out of the pale of the Church.

"When we see some Authors in the Reformation afford Heaven to persons that never professed Christ, this is spiritual prodigality, and beyond that liberality which we consider now; for, Christ is ours; and where we can apply him, we can give all comforts in him; But none to others. Not that we manacle the hands of God, or say God can save no man without the profession of Christ, But that God hath put nothing else into his Churche's hands to save men by, but Christ delivered in his Scripture, applied in the preaching of the Gospel, and sealed in the Sacraments. And therefore, if we should give this comfort to any but those that received him, and received him so, according to his ordinance in his Church, we should be over-liberall, for we should give more than our owne." [56]

In another sermon Donne also declared that to him the only way of salvation was through Christ, as revealed in the Gospel, as preached by His Church, and that he was not curious to inquire how those men were saved who never had Christ preached to them, and had not the Christian Church established amongst themselves.[57]

"To me, to whom God hath revealed his Son, in a Gospel, by a Church, there can be no way of salvation but by applying that Son of God, by that Gospel, in that

[55] *XXVI Sermons*, 25.
[56] *LXXX Sermons*, 75.
[57] Donne emphasized the need of conversion and preaching of the Gospel among those nations which had never heard of Christ. His sermon preached to the Honourable Company of the Virginian Plantation (1622) has been claimed to be the first missionary sermon ever preached in England. He said that the real glory of the colonization of Virginia would consist in preaching the Gospel to the heathen there. "Preach to them Doctrinally, preach to them Practically; Enamour them with your *Justice,* and (as farre as may consist with your security) your *civilitie;* but inflame them with your *godliness,* and your *Religion.* Bring them to *love* and *Reverence* the name of that *King,* that sends men to teach them the wayes of Civilitie in this world, but to *feare* and *adore* the Name of that *King of Kings,* that sends men to teach them the waies of Religion, for the next world."

Church. Nor is there any other foundation for any, nor other name by which any can be saved, but the name of Jesus. But how this foundation is presented, and how this name of Jesus is notified to them, amongst whom there is no Gospel preached, no Church established I am not curious in inquiring. I know God can be as mercifull as those tender Fathers present him to be; and I would be as charitable as they are. And therefore humbly imbracing that manifestation of his Son, which he hath afforded me, I leave God, to his unsearchable waies of working upón others, without further inquisition." [58]
But he, with certain Fathers, hoped that those Pagan Philosophers, like Socrates and Plato, who had taught virtue, and had themselves lived in a godly manner, might be saved.

"As those blessed Fathers of tender bowels, . . . so did they inlarge this mercy farther, and carry it even to the Gentiles, to the Pagans that had no knowledge of Christ in any established Church. You shall not finde *Trismegistus,* a *Numa Pompilius,* a *Plato,* a *Socrates,* for whose salvation you shall not find some Father or some Ancient and Reverend Author, an advocate."
He shared the hope of the blessed Fathers that these Pagan Philosophers might be saved.

Donne, as we have seen, as a controversialist, theologian and Anglican Divine, shows a breadth of vision, tolerance and Christian Charity, combined with vast sacred and profane learning and intimate knowledge of the human soul, with its infirmities as well as its infinite capacity for divine love and compassion which entitles him to an eminent place, like that of Hooker and Bishop Andrewes, in the history of the Anglican Church.

[58] *LXXX Sermons,* 26.

CHAPTER III

REVEALED theology is that science of God and divine things which, objectively, is based on supernatural revelation, and subjectively, is treated in the light of Christian faith. Revealed theology thus deals with theoretical truths of faith concerning God and His works, and is called *dogmata fidei,* while moral theology is *dogmata morum,* and is confined to the consideration of practical truths of morality.

As God is the primary object and the first principle of Christian theology, revealed theology begins with the doctrine of God's existence, essence and attributes. The dogma of the threefold personality of God is the fundamental element in the Christian doctrine of God, and therefore the Trinity, its nature, office and attributes are thoroughly discussed in revealed theology. This is followed by considering God in relation to His external activity which consists in :

(1) Creation, which is His first expression of external activity ; and
(2) Redemption through Christ ;

thus the last section also includes the Incarnation and Christology.

We have divided this chapter under the following headings :

(1) The Doctrine of God.
(2) Creation.
(3) The Holy Trinity.
(4) Christology.
(5) The Incarnation.
(6) Christ and the Holy Ghost.
(7) Christ and the Virgin Mary.
(8) The Resurrection and the Ascension.
(9) Angels.

Donne has not discussed in a systematic way the nature, attributes, or the Christian conception of God in one treatise, and therefore his conception of God, as creator, Saviour, and Lover has to be pieced together from the whole body of his sermons. To Donne the attribute of God is His Being; the being of God distinguishes Him from those of His creatures.

> " Howsoever, all intend, that this is a name that denotes Essence, Being: Being is the name of God, and of God onely." [1]

Donne quotes Plato in support of this definition of God: " Plato saies well, *Ejus nomen est potius non esse;* the name of the Creator is, *I am,* but of every creature rather, I am not, I am nothing." [1] He points out that the Platonian conception of the difference between the being of God and the being of man is philosophically sound.

> " Man hath more privations than positives in him; Man hath but his own being; Man hath not the being of an Angel, nor the being of a lyon; God hath all in a kind of eminence more excellently than the kinds them-selves, . . . Man had an eternall not being before; that is before the creation; for those infinite millions of millions of generations before the Creation, there was a God, whose name was *I am.*" [2]

Donne argues that as man had an eternal ' not being ' before his creation, and would have had an eternal not being after his dissolution by death, in soul as well as in body, if God had not made his soul immortal by preserving the being that He had imprinted in it at creation. Thus man's life is a continual change that tends towards not being, while the being of God is eternal, which is signified by His name *I am.*

Another important attribute of God is His universality, and His omnipresence.

> " How often God admits into his owne Name, this addition of universality, *Omne, All,* as though he would be knowne by that especially. He is omnipresent, There he can doe all; He is omniscient, There he can know all; He is omnipresent, There he can direct all. Neither doth God extend himself to all, that he may gather from all, but that he may gather all, and all might meet in him, and enjoy him." [3]

God works perfectly in all, because He sees all and knows all.

> " The Sunne works upon things that he sees not (as Mynes in the wombe of the earth) and so works the lesse

[1] *LXXX Sermons,* 5.
[2] *Ibid.*
[3] *LXXX Sermons,* 68.

perfectly.   God sees all, and works upon all, and desires
perfection in all." [4]
He declared that God is not omnipresent in a manner that
He is an angel in an Angel, and a stone in a stone, and so on,
but His omnipresence is independent of all these limitations.

" But God is truly so omnipresent, as that he is with us
before he comes to us . . . why doe I pray that thou
wouldst come into me, who could not only not pray, but
could not bee, if thou were not in me before? " [5]

The supreme attribute of God is His communicableness, His
desire to be known by all who seek Him.   Without this
attribute God would have dwelt in lonely, far off regions, in
all His majesty, but there would have been no communion
between God and Man.

" Our first step in this first part, is the *sociablenesse,* the
communicablenesse of God;   He loves holy meetings, he
loves the *communion of saints, the household of the faith-
full* . . . sayes Solomon, *his delight is to be with the son*s
of men, and that the sons of men should be with him . . .
very good *grammarians* amongst the *Hebrews,* have
thought, and said, that that *name,* by which God notifies
himself to the world, in the very beginning of *Genesis,*
which is *Elohim,* as it is a plurall word there so it hath no
singular: they say we cannot name God, but plurally;   so
sociable, so communicable, so extensive, so derivative of
himself, is God, and so manifold are the beames, and the
emanations that flow out from him." [6]

God is accessible to all and it is not the purpose of God to deny
himself to anyone.

" But it is a precept of Accessibleness, and of Affability;
Affability, that is, a civility of the city of God, and a courtship of the Court of heaven, to receive other men, the
Images of God, with the same easiness that God receives
you. . . . God is no inaccessible God, that he may not be
spoken to . . . nor dilatory, that he does not that he does
seasonably." [7]

God promises this " flowing out of the Holy Ghost upon all,"
because it is an attribute of His goodness.

[4] *LXXX Sermons,* 67.
[5] *LXXX Sermons,* 7.
[6] *L Sermons,* 32.
[7] *XXVI Sermons,* 3.

" It agrees with the nature of goodness to be so diffusive, communicable to all. It agrees with the nature of God, who is goodnesse," [8]

to be accessible to all. The goodness of God comes before His greatness.

" He is All greatnesse, but he is All Goodnesse first : He comes to shew his Greatnesse at last, but yet his Goodnesse begins his Name, and can never be worne out in his Nature," [9]

and lastly, Majesty and not Force is an attribute of the Christian God for " our God is the God of peace, and of sweetnesse; spirituall peace, spirituall honey to our souls." [10]

Donne declared that we cannot know God through the *via negativa* of pseudo-Dionysius the Areopagite.

" Canst thou rely and lean upon so inferior a knowledge, as is delivered by negations? And because a devout speculative man (Dionysius) hath said *Negationes de Deo sunt veræ affirmationes autem sunt inconvenientes,* will it serve thy turn to hear that God is that which can not be named, can not be comprehended, or which is nothing else, when every negation implies some privation, which can not be safely enough admitted in God." [11]

God cannot be truly *represented* by His attributes such as " good, just, wise," since these words can never be used without implying wiser, and more just, or if we call Him best or some such phrase, then " highest degree respects some lower, and mean one, and are these in God? " [11] Donne seems to be echoing S. Thomas Aquinas. S. Thomas held that these names of God cannot represent Him as one being can represent another of the same species or genus as itself, but rather as the principle whose effects they are and in regard to whom " the effects are defective."

" As regards absolute and affirmative names of God, as *good, wise,* and the like, various and many opinions have been given . . . the aforesaid names signify the Divine Substance, but in an imperfect manner, as creatures also represent It imperfectly. So when we say, God is good, the

[8] *LXXX Sermons,* 37.
[9] *LXXX Sermons,* 42.
[10] *Ibid.*
[11] *Essays,* p. 51.

meaning is not, God is the cause of goodness, or God is not bad; but the meaning is, whatever good we attribute to creatures, pre-exists in God, and in a more excellent and higher way. Hence it does not follow that God is good, because He causes goodness; but rather, on the contrary, He causes goodness in things because He is Himself good, according to what Augustine says, *Because He is good, we are.*" [12]

Donne thinks that it is not enough to know God in His awful majesty in His Loneliness, or in His great incomprehensible Powers, for the prime attribute of the Christian God is His desire to communicate with Man.

" For it is not enough to find *Deum,* a God; a great and incomprehensible power, that sits *in luce,* in light, but *in luce inaccessibli,* in light that we can not comprehend. A God that enjoys his owne eternity, his own peace, his own blessedness, but respects not us, reflects not upon us, communicates nothing to us." [13]

The Christian conception of God is that of the Father of all creatures who sheds His glory not only on the soul of man but also on all His creation.

" God is *Pater luminum* the Father of lights. Whether we take lights there to be *Angels,* created with the light (some take it so) or to be the severall lights set up in the heavens, Sun and Moon and Stars (some take it so) or to be the light of Grace in infusion by the Spirit or the light of the Church in manifestation, by the *Word* . . . God is the Father of lights, of all lights, but so he is of raine, and clouds, too. And God is the Father of glory. . . . From that inglorious drop of raine, that falls into the dust, and rises no more, to those glorious Saints who shall rise from the dust and fall no more, but as they arise at once to the fulnesse of *Essential* joy, so arise daily in *accidental* joyes, all are the children of God, and are alike of kin to us." [14]

CREATION

Donne, like S. Augustine and S. Thomas Aquinas, held that the world was created out of nothing.

" To make our approaches nearer, and better effectually

[12] *Sum. Theol.,* I, qu. 13, Art. 2.
[13] *LXXX Sermons,* 74.
[14] *L Sermons,* 41.

let him that will not confess this nothing assign something of which the world was made. If it be of itself, it is God; and it is God, if it be of God; who is also so simple [15] that it is impossible to imagine anything before him of which he should be compounded, of any workman to do it. For to say, as one doth [16] that the world might be eternal, and yet not be God, because God's eternity is all at once, and the World's successive, will not reconcile it; for yet some part of the world must be as old as God, and infinite things are equal and equal to God are God.[17]

He affirmed with S. Thomas Aquinas " That it is an article of our belief that the world began." [18]   Donne conceives, like Plato, that God created the physical world according to a definite *Idea* and pattern which He had of it in Himself from eternity.

" God himself made all that he made according to a pattern. God had deposited and laid up in himselfe certaine formes, patternes, Ideas of everything that he made. He made nothing of which he had not preconceived the forme, and pre-determined in himselfe, I will make it thus. And when he had made anything, he saw it was good; good because it answered the pattern, the Image; good, because it was like to that. And therefore . . . God pronounced they were good, because they were presently like their pattern, that is, like that forme, which was in him for them." [19]

Donne has quoted with approval the following conception of Creation of S. Thomas Aquinas, who thought that the greatest dignity of creation was that its *Idea* was eternal in God.

[15] This conception of God's simplicity, Donne seems to have borrowed from S. Thomas Aquinas, who in considering the proposition that we can know God only by knowing "what he is not" declared: "Moreover it is possible to show in what manner God is not by removing from him those qualities which cannot fitly be attributed to him, such as composition, motion, and others of this sort. First, therefore, we must inquire concerning his simplicity, through which composition is removed from him. And because whatever corporeal things are simple are also imperfect and are parts of other things." *Sum. Theol.,* Part I, qu. 3.
[16] Boethius, *De Consolatione,* 5 Pros. 6, Donne's marginal reference.
[17] *Essays,* p. 72.
[18] *Essays* 37, *Sum. Theol.,* Part I, qu. 42, Art. 2. Donne here calls S. Thomas " Another instrument and engine of thine, whom thou hadst so enabled that nothing was too mineral nor centric for the search and reach of his wit."
[19] *L Sermons,* 29.

" The greatest dignity which we can give this world is, that the idea of it is eternal and was ever in God, and that he knew this world, not only *Scientia intellectus,* by which he knows things which shall never be, and are in his purpose impossible, though yet possible and contingent to us, but after failing became also to our knowledge impossible (as it is yet possible you will read this book through now, but if you discontinue it, which is in your liberty it is then impossible to your knowledge, and was ever so to God's) but as also *Scientia visionis,* by which he knows only infallible things, and therefore these ideas and eternal impressions in God, may boldly be said to be God, for nothing understands God of itself, but God." [20]

Donne says that when God made Heaven and Earth God only said " create," " so that that which was made *sine sermone,* without speaking, was only matter without form, heaven without light, and earth without any productive virtue or disposition, to bring forth, and to nourish creatures." [21] This was the first stage in creation—creation of Matter without Form. The second stage was the creation of Matter with specific forms.

" But when God came to those specifique forms, and to those creatures wherein he would be sensibly glorified after, they were made *in sermone,* by his word ; . . . God spake and so all things were made ; Light and Firmament, Land and Sea, Plants and Beasts, and Fishes, and Fowls were made all *in sermone,* by his word." [21]

But the creation of Man was the work of the Trinity, it was done through consultation, according to a definite plan and divine pattern.

" But when God came to the best of his creatures, to Man, Man was not only made *in Verbo,* as the rest were, by speaking a word, but by consultation, by a conference, by a counsell, *faciamus hominem, let us make Man;* there is a more express manifestation of divers persons speaking together, of a concurrence of the Trinity." [22]

In another sermon Donne declared that Nature was created

---

[20] *Essays,* p. 73. This paragraph is derived from *Summa Theologica* of S. Thomas Aquinas, Part I, qu. 14.
[21] *XXVI Sermons,* 13.
[22] *Ibid.*

E

not by God Himself, but the spirit or Power emanating from God, and that only Man was made in the Image of God.

" The spirit of God in this place is something proceeding from God, but it is not God himself. . . . That this spirit of God may be the universall power, which sustaines and inanimates the whole world, which the Platoniques have called the *Soule of the World,* and others intend by the name of Nature. . . ." [23]

Though Man was created out of Matter, he was made by God in His own Image.

" That we are made according to a pattern, to an image, to a likenesse, which God proposed to himselfe for the making of Man.   This consideration that God did not rest, in that pre-existent matter, out of which he made all other creatures, and produced their formes, out of their matter, for the making of Man; but took a forme, a patterne, a modell for that work, this is the north winde, that is called upon to carry out the perfumes of the garden, to spread the goodnesse of God abroad." [24]

The " highest elevation " of man is that he is different from the rest of the creation, that he has " another forme, another image, another likenesse." [24]

Donne conceives the creation of the universe as proceeding in well defined stages to the divine purpose of final revelation of God-in-man, that is, Christ.

" We see, God drew persons nearer to him (meaning the Trinity), then Sunne, or Moon, or Starres, or anything which is visible, and discernible to us, he created Angels . . . so far was God from being alone." [25]

God manifested Himself in creation; it was a revelation of His glory.

" Since *God* himself, who *so* many millions of ages contented himself with *himself* in Heaven, yet at last made this world for his glory." [26]

But man was created so that he may uphold the divine glory.

" Hath God made this world as his Theatre . . . that man

[23] *LXXX Sermons,* 31.
[24] *L Sermons,* 28.
[25] *L Sermons,* 32.
[26] *XXVI Sermons,* 24.

may represent God in his conversation; and wilt thou play no part ? "[27]

The glory of creation should lead us to the love of God for,
  " What is there in this world immediately and primarily worthy our love, which (by acceptation) is worthy the love of God ? *Earth* and *Heaven* are but the foot-stool of God." [28]

Thus God was not satisfied with " this visible and discernible world," [29] and he endowed man with a reasonable soul and gave him " a nature already above all other creatures, and a nature capable of a better than his owne is yet (for, by his precious Promise we are made partakers of the Divine Nature). We are made *Semen Dei*. The seed of God, borne of God, *Genus Dei*, The off-spring of God, *Idem spiritus cum Domino*, The same spirit with the Lord; He the same flesh with us, and we the same spirit with him." [30]

The only reason for making man in His own Image was that God was in love with the soul of man.
  " All in all, is from the love of God; but there is something for God to love; there is a man, there is a soule in that man, there is a will in that soule, and God is in love with this man, and this soule, and this will and would have it. . . ." [31]

Donne in an eloquent passage describes how God seeks the soul of the individual, how He chases it with His love, and how numerous are the testimonies of this eternal seeking of God !
  " . . . he sought thee before that, in the catalogue of all his Creatures, where he might have left thee a stone, or a plant, or a beast, and then he gave thee an immortal soul, capable of all his future blessings; yea, before this he sought thee, when thou wast no where, nothing, he brought thee then, the greatest step of all, from being nothing, to be a Creature." [32]

Then God was seeking the Christian soul among the heathen, the Gentiles and the heretical sects.

[27] *XXVI Sermons*, 24.
[28] *Essays*, p. 88.
[29] *L Sermons*, 32.
[30] *LXXX Sermons*, 62.
[31] *LXXX Sermons*, 31.
[32] *XXVI Sermons*, 18.

" Thus early had he sought thee in the Church amongst
hypocrites; out of the Church amongst the Heathen; In
his Creatures amongst creatures of an ignoble nature, and
in the first vacuity, when thou wast nothing, he sought thee
so early as in Adam, so early in the book of life, and when
wilt thou think it a fit time to seek him ? " [32]

Donne has pointed out that there are mainly three ways of
knowing God :

(1) God in Nature.
(2) God in the Scriptures and the Sacraments.
(3) God in Christ.

As the world is " God's manifestation of himself," [33] it is
possible for a natural man to have a glimpse of God in nature.
Everything in creation calls man to God.

" Here God shewes this in considerate man, his book of
creatures, which he may run and reade; and yet see that
every creature calls him to a consideration of God.   Every
Art that he sees, asks him, where had I this prudence, and
industry.   Every flower that he sees asks him, where had I
this beauty, this fragrancy, this medicinall vertue in me? " [34]

Donne says that " there is light enough in this dawning of the
day," and such admirable order, and correspondence of
various parts in creation that the intellect of the natural man
unaided by His word can discern God in nature.

" The correspondence and relation of all parts of Nature
to one Author, the continuity and dependance of every
piece and joynt of this frame of the world, the admirable
order, the immutable succession, the lively and certain
generation, and birth of effects from their Parents, the
Causes : in all these, though there be no sound, no voice,
yet we may even see that it is an excellent song, an
admirable piece of musick and harmony; and that God
does (as it were) play upon this Organ in his administration
and providence by naturall means and instruments ; and so
there is some kind of creation in us, some knowledge of God

---

[33] *LXXX Sermons*, 21.
[34] *LXXX Sermons*.   Donne seems to divide Man into three cate-
gories :
(1) Natural man, who is the moral man without faith.
(2) Christian, is the man of faith, that is, the man who has accepted
the revelation of Christ.
(3) The regenerate Christian is one who has experienced illumination.

imprinted, *sine sermone,* without any relation to his word." [35]

The knowledge thus obtained through natural means is an uncertain light, on which we should not rely for guidance.

"But this is a Creation as of heaven and earth, which were dark and empty, and without form, till the spirit of God moved, and till God spoke : till there came the Spirit, the breath of God's mouth, the word of God, it is but a faint twilight, it is but an uncertaine glimmering, which we have of God in the creature." [36]

The light of nature, unaided by the light of faith, is uncertain because the natural understanding, if it is to discern God must be free from all earthly passion, a state of mind which is very difficult to attain.

"The light of naturall understanding, that which *Plinie* calls *serenitatem animi,* when the mind of man, disencumbered of all Eclipses, and all clouds of passion, or inordinate love of earthly things, is enlightened so far, as to discern God in nature." [37]

Every creature shows God "as a glass, but glimeringly and transitorily, by the frailty both of the receiver and beholder." The knowledge of God derived from reason and natural religion can only help us "to know what he *doth,* not what he *is.*" It is the knowledge of His activity or effects and not of His Essence. Faith and not reason can fully comprehend God, "For all acquired knowledge is by degrees, and successive; but God is impartible, and only faith which can receive it all at once can comprehend him." [38] In the "discovery of God's Essence" [38] reason is powerless to assist us. S. Thomas Aquinas also maintained that we can only know the effects of God, but not His Essence through natural reason, for our knowledge begins from sense and can go so far as it can be led by sensible things, but our mind cannot see the Essence of God, because the "effects of God do not equal the power of God as their cause."

"But because they are his effect and depend on their cause, we can be led from them as far as to know that God exists, and to know of him what must necessarily belong to

[35] *XXVI Sermons,* 13.
[36] *Ibid.*
[37] *LXXX Sermons,* 39.
[38] *Essays in Divinity,* pp. 48–50.

him as the First Cause of all things exceedings all things caused by him." [39]

Another revelation of God is in His Scriptures which Donne calls the " face of Jesus Christ," it is here that the will of God is clearly manifested to us.

> " But in *sermone,* in his word, when we come to him in his Scriptures, we finde better and nobler creatures produced in us, clearer notions of God, and more evident manifestations of his power, and of his goodness towards us." [40]

Though the Scriptures are one of the means of salvation, they should be strengthened by administration of the Sacraments in a visible Church.

> " So then thy meanes are the Scriptures; That is thy evidence; but then this evidence must be sealed to thee in the Sacraments " [41]

as administered by the Church, which is the repository of the Spirit of Christ.

> " Now beloved, this Knowledge, as it is opposed to inconsideration, is in this, that God by breeding us in the visible Church multiplies unto us so many helps and assistances in the word preached, in the Sacraments, in other sacramentall and Rituall, and ceremoniall things," [42]

which though they are " auxiliary, subsidiary " things, strengthen our steadfastness on the path of virtue, and our love for Christ.

Donne explains how the relation of the Christian to God differs from that of the natural man, and in what sense Christ is " our Jehovah."

> " To the naturall man, God gives generall notions of himselfe; a God that spreads over all as the heavens; a God that sustains all as the earth; a God that transports, and communicates all to all as the sea : But to the Christian Church God applies himself in more particular notions, as a Father, as a Son, as a holy Ghost. And to every Christian

---

[39] *Sum. Theol.,* I, qu. 12, Art. 12.
[40] *XXVI Sermons,* 13.
[41] *LXXX Sermons,* 23.
[42] *LXXX Sermons,* 30. Donne also points out that these visible assistances which the Church gives us must be confirmed in our own conscience, " the Abridgement of all Nature, and all Law, his owne heart and conscience."

soule, as a Creator, a Redeemer, a Benefactor . . . my present Being in this world, and my eternal Being in the next, is made knowne to me by his name of *Jehovah,* the God of all Being, which is the foundation of all his other attributes, and includes all his other names. . . . Now that which *Jehovah* was to *David, Jesus* is to us. Man in generall hath relation to God, as he is *Jehovah,* Being; we have relation to Christ as he is *Jesus,* our salvation; Salvation is our Being, *Jesus* is our *Jehovah.*" [43]

THE HOLY TRINITY

But a belief in the *Trinity,* as the threefold manifestation of God as the Father, the Son, and the Holy Ghost, is essential for the full and complete comprehension of God.

" To believe in God, one great, one universall, one infinite power, does but distinguish us from beasts; For there are no men that do not acknowledge such a Power, or that do not believe in it, if they acknowledge it; . . . But that which distinguishes man from man, that which onely makes his Immortality a blessing is to conceive aright of the Power of the Father, of the wisdome of the Son, of the Goodness of the Holy Ghost; of the Mercie of the Father, of the Merits of the Son, of the Application of the Holy Ghost; of the creation of the Father, of the Redemption of the Son, of the Sanctification of the Holy Ghost. Without this, all notions of God are but confused, all worship of God is but Idolatry, all confession of God is but Atheisme. . . ." [44]

He thought it was easier to comprehend God through the Trinity.

" The generall notion of a mighty God, may lesse fit my particular purposes. But I coine my gold into current money, when I apprehend God, in the severall notions of the Trinity." [45]

Donne believed that it was the effect of faith, the operation

---

[43] *LXXX Sermons,* 50.

[44] *LXXX Sermons,* 44.

[45] *L Sermons.* Elsewhere he declared that knowledge of God through Philosophy is inadequate when compared to the belief of God in the Trinity. "Let him have writ as much as *Aristotle* writ, or as is written upon *Aristotle,* which is multiplication enough; yet he hath not learnt to spel, that hath not learnt the Trinity; not learnt to pronounce the first word that cannot bring three persons into one God."

of the Holy Ghost, which creates in us a sincere belief in the
Trinity, natural reason and the knowledge of the Scriptures
were not enough in themselves.

" The principall use and office of my knowledge,[46] is to
know the Trinity, for to know an unity in the Godhead,
that there is but one God, naturall reason serves our turn.
. . . For if this knowledge might be had without Scriptures,
why should not the heathen believe the Trinity, as well as I,
since they lack no naturall faculties which Christians have?
And if the Scriptures themselves, without the operation of
the Holy Ghost should bring this clearnesse, why should not
the Jews and the Arians conform themselves to this doctrine
of the Trinity, as well as I, since they accept those
Scriptures, out of which I prove the Trinity to mine own
Conscience? We must then attend his working in us; we
must not admit such a vexation of Spirit, as either to vex
our Spirit, or the Spirit of God, by inquiring further than
he hath been pleased to reveale." [47]

The three persons of the Trinity Donne calls " so many
handles by which we may take hold of God," [48] but it shall not
be possible for us to comprehend God alone in all His infinite
attributes.

" And as wee can not take hold of a torch by the light,
but by the staffe we may; so though we can not take hold
of God, as God, who is incomprehensible, and inappre-
hensible, yet as a Father, as a Son, as a Spirit, dwelling in
us, we can. There is nothing in Nature that can fully
represent and bring home the notion of the Trinity to
us. . . ." [49]

As the knowledge of the Trinity is due to the Spirit of God
working in us, the Platonic philosophers, the Jews, and the
Muslims also have a glimmering of the knowledge of the
Trinity.[50]

[46] By knowledge he means the knowledge which is created in us by the
Holy Ghost.
[47] *LXXX Sermons,* 30.
[48] *LXXX Sermons,* 38.
[49] *Ibid.*
[50] Donne's reference to the Platonic philosophers' conception of the
Trinity is interesting because later in the seventeenth century the
Cambridge Platonists like Henry More and Cudworth elaborated this
point in detail. " Hence is it, that in the books of the Platonique philosophers, and in others, much ancienter than they, (if the books of Hermes

THE ATTRIBUTES AND OFFICES OF THE TRINITY

Donne assigns the three attributes of God, Power, Wisdom and Goodness to the three Persons of the Trinity respectively, though he is careful to point out that they all subsist in each Person jointly, for " they are all (as we say in the Schoole) *Co-omnipotents,* they have a joynt-Almightnesse, a joynt-Wisdome, and a joynt-Goodnesse." [51] Donne says that Power is the attribute of God.

" The roote of all, Independent, not proceeding from any other, as both the other Persons do, and Power and Sovereignty best resembles that Independency, therefore we attribute Power to the Father." [51]

As Christ proceeds from the Father, *per modum intellectus,* his principal attribute is wisdom.

" That as our understanding proceeds from our reasonable soule, so the second person, the Son, proceeds from the Father, therefore we attribute wisdome to the Son." [51]

The Holy Ghost proceeds *per modum voluntatis.*

" That as our soule (as the roote) and our understanding, proceeding from that Soule, produce our will, and the object of our will is evermore *Bonum,* that which is good in our apprehension, therefore we attribute to the Holy Ghost, Goodnesse." [52]

According to Donne there are three faculties of the Soul, understanding, will and memory, and these respectively correspond to the three persons of the Trinity.

" So then in this first naturall faculty of the soule, the understanding, stands the Image, of the first Person, the Father, Power : and in the second faculty which is the will, is the Image, the Attribute of the second Person the Sonne, which is Wisdome : for wisdome is not so much in knowing, in understanding, as in electing, in choosing, in assenting. . . . And then, in the third faculty of the Soule, the Memory,

Trismegistus, and others, be as ancient as is pretended in their behalfe) we finde as cleare expressing of the Trinity as in the old Testament, at least. And hence is it, that in the Talmud of the Jews, and in the Alcoran of the Turks, though they oppose the Trinity, yet when they handle not that point, there fall often from them, as cleare confessions of the three Persons, as from any of those Philosophers, who were altogether disinterested in that Controversie " (*LXXX Sermons,* 38).

[51] *LXXX Sermons,* 41.
[52] *Ibid.*

is the Image of the third person, the Holy Ghost, that is, Goodnesse. For to remember, to recollect our former understanding, and our assenting, so far as to doe them, to crowne them with action, that's true goodnesse." [53]

Donne considers that as the three Persons of the Trinity have different attributes, so there are certain sins which offend the several Persons particularly. He says that as there is one Godhead, so all sin is against God, but there are various sins which are against *Power, Wisdom* and *Goodness,* that is, against the Father, the Son, and the Holy Ghost, for the classification of these sins, Donne follows the Schoolmen.

" For branches, the Schoolmen have named three couples, which they have called *sins against the holy Ghost,* because naturally they shut out those means by which the Holy Ghost might work upon us. The first couple is, *presumption* and *desperation;* for presumption takes away the feare of God, and desperation the love of God. And then, they name *Impenitence,* and *hardnesse* of heart; for Impenitence removes all sorrow for sins past, and hardnesse of heart all tendernesse towards future tentations. And lastly, they name the *resisting of a truth acknowledged before,* and the *envying of other men, who have made better use of God's Grace than we have done;* for this resisting of a Truth, is a shuting up of ourselves against it, and this envying of others, is a Sorrow, that that Truth should prevaile upon them." [54]

As to the offices of the Trinity, Donne believes that all the three Persons concur in their judgments. In the judgment of Election and Reprobation, in the second judgment, that is, its execution in the visible Church, and in the last judgment which shall decide the fate of the soul either for eternal glory or everlasting condemnation, all the three Persons are equal judges.

" In all these three judgments, all the three Persons of the Trinity are judges. Consider God altogether, and so in all outward works, all the Trinity concurres, because all are but *one* God." [55]

But as in Christ the divine and human natures have been blended together, Christ executes His judgment in flesh, and

[53] *L Sermons,* 29.
[54] *LXXX Sermons,* 35.
[55] *L Sermons,* 12.

not only as a creative spirit, for the human nature is as much a part of His Person as the divine element in Him.

" Now all things our Saviour Christ Jesus exercises either *per carnem,* or at least *in carne.* Whatsoever the Father does, the Sonne does too *in carne,* because now there is an unseparable union betwixt God and the humane nature : The Father creates new souls every day in the inanimation of children, and the Sonne creates them with him ; The Father concurs with all second causes as the first moving cause of all naturall things, and all this the Sonne does too, but all this *in carne.* Though he be in our human flesh, he is not the less able to doe the acts belonging to the God-head, but *per carnem,* by the flesh instrumentally, visibly, he executes judgment, because he is the Son of man, God hath been so indulgent to man, as that there should be no judgment given upon man but man should give it." [56]

CHRISTOLOGY

Christ—the Second Person in the Trinity—The Incarnation

We shall deal with Christology under the following headings :
(1) The Incarnation.
(2) Pre-existence of Christ or Christ as Logos.
(3) The Consubstantiality of Christ.
(4) The Person and Nature of Christ.
(5) Heresies about His Nature.
The extent of God's love for man and the power of divinity inherent in His Nature was fully revealed when God assumed human nature in the person of Jesus Christ.

" But it is a God, that is *Deus noster ;* ours, as we are his creatures ; ours, as we are like him, made to his image ; ours, as he hath descended to us in his Incarnation ; and ours as we are ascended with him in his glorification. So that wee do not consider, as our God, except we come to the consideration of God in Christ, God and Man." [57]

[56] *L Sermons,* 12. Hooker also says : " Finally, sith God hath deified our nature, though not by turning it into himself, yet by making it his own inseparable habitation, we cannot now conceive how God should without man either exercise Divine power, or receive the glory of Divine praise. For man is in both an associate of Deity " (*Ecc. Pol.,* Bk. V, Chap. LIV).
[57] *LXXX Sermons,* 74.

Donne argues that the knowledge of God as separate from His Revelation in Christ is not enough for the Christian, for the Jews also possess it; God's fullest revelation has been in Christ and therefore the knowledge of the Incarnation is essential for the knowledge of God.

" Naturall apprehensions of God, though those naturall apprehensions may have much subtlety, voluntary elections of a Religion, though those voluntary elections have much singularity, morall directions for life, though those morall directions may have much severity, are all frivolous, and lost, if all determine not in Christianity, in the notion of God, so as God hath manifested and conveyed himself to us; in God the Father, God the Son, and God the Holy Ghost. . . ." [58]

He approvingly quotes the saying of the apostle that " *when you are without Christ, you were without God.*" [58]   Donne says that there would have been no revelation of the mystery of the Trinity without the Incarnation.

" The manifestation of the mysterie of the Trinity was reserved for Christ.   Some intimation in the old, but the publication only in the New Testament; some irradiations in the Law, but the illustration onely in the Gospell; some emanation of beames, as of the sun before it is got above the Horizon, in the Prophets, but the glorious proceeding thereof, and the attaining to a meridinall height, only in the Evangelists." [59]

The central fact in the history of the divine revelation is the Incarnation; it was the realization of the prophecies and promises which had been given to the Old Testament prophets.

" The other act of his mercy enwrapped in this word, *veni, I came,* is this, that he that came to the old world but in promises, and prophecies, and figures, is actually, really, personally, and presentially come to us; of which difference, that man will have the best sense, who languishes under the heavy expectation of a reversion, in office, or inheritance or hath felt the joy of coming to the actuall possession of such a reversion." [60]

[58] *LXXX Sermons,* 44.
[59] *LXXX Sermons,* 28.
[60] *LXXX Sermons,* 7.

Though by the Incarnation the nature and the glory of the Father has not suffered any diminution, for He is not subject to any change, the nature of man has received the full dignity and perfection of which it was capable. Donne says that we should consider,

"the dignity, that the nature of man received in that union wherein this *Lord* was thus made this Christ, for, the Godhead did not swallow the manhood; but man, that nature remained still. The greater kingdom did not swallow the less . . ." [61]

Hooker also says,

"The very cause of his taking upon him our nature was to change it, to better the quality, and to advance the condition thereof, although in no sort to abolish the substance which he took nor to infuse into it the natural forces and properties of his Deity. . . . God from us can receive nothing, we by him have obtained much. For albeit the natural properties of Deity be not communicable to man's nature, the supernatural gifts, graces, and effects thereof are." [62]

The Pre-existence and Consubstantiality of Christ

There are several passages in Donne's sermons where he refers to Christ as Logos, and declares that Christ existed before the beginning of the world, that He appeared in figures and promises to the prophets of the Old Testament, and that He was present with His Father at the creation of the universe.[63]

"Christ was never in minority, never under years; there was never any time when he was not as ancient as the Ancient of Days, as old as his Father." [64]

He held that Christ existed "before all beginnings, and to be still the Image of the Father," that He was an exact image of the Father, co-eternal with Him.

"God had a picture of himself from all eternity; from all eternity, the Sonne of God was the Image of the invisible God." [65]

Donne says,

[61] *LXXX Sermons*, 40.
[62] *Ecc. Pol.*, Bk. V.
[63] As Tertullian said: "The whole order of the Divine administration had its course through him."
[64] *L Sermons*, 3.
[65] *LXXX Sermons*, 65.

"Christ was the Lamb slain from the beginning of the world; appointed for a sacrifice from the first promise of a Messias in Paradise long before that; from all eternity." [66] He rejected the Arian heresy that there was a time when Christ did not exist, and therefore He was created and thus became a creature.

"The Arians who say . . . there was a time when Christ was not, intimating that he had a beginning, and therefore was a creature, yet they will allow that he was created before the generall creation, and so, assisted at ours, but he was infinite generations before that, in the bosome of his Father, at our Election. . . ." [67]

Donne believed that Christ was of the same divine uncreated substance as the Father and therefore truly a God, and that He was co-eternal in existence with the Father. He says "The Father and Son are but one roote," [68] and "that both Father and Son are but one beginning" [68] and that "co-eternity enwraps alike" [69] all the three Persons of the Trinity.

The Nature of Christ and the Heresies about His Person

As Hooker has pointed out there are four things "which concur to make the whole state of our Lord Jesus Christ" [70]; His Deity, His manhood, the union of both, and the destruction of the divine and human being joined in one. And there have been four principal heresies, one pertaining to each definite aspect of Christ's nature. Arian heresy against the Deity of Christ, Apollinarians against His Humanity; while Nestorians tried to separate Him into two distinct persons, and the followers of Eutyches confounded in His Person the two natures which one should distinguish. Against these four main heresies, there have been four general councils; the Council of Nice against Arians, the Council of Constantinople against Apollinarians, the Council of Ephesus against Nestorians, the Chalcedon Council against Eutychians. The Anglican Church is free from all these heresies. Donne has emphasized the fact that in order to have a true conception of the nature of Christ we must recognize the divine as well as

[66] *LXXX Sermons,* 7.
[67] *L Sermons,* 14.
[68] *LXXX Sermons,* 34.
[69] *LXXX Sermons,* 28.
[70] *Ecc. Pol.,* Bk. V, Chap. IV.

the human in Him, and the perfect union of both in His Person.

"So then the hypostaticall union of the Godhead to the humane nature, in his conception, made him *Christ*, for . . . then in that union of the two natures, *did God anoint him with the oyle of gladness above his fellows. . . .*" [71]

Donne held that we cannot exalt the divine in Christ at the expense of the human, for we shall be neglecting the main object of the Incarnation which was "to redeem Man," [71] but by becoming Man Christ's divinity did not suffer any loss, though human nature received great dignity. The glory of Christ consists as much in His Humanity as in His Divinity.

"But Christ is so made of God and Man, as that he is man still, for all the glory of the Deity, and God still, for all the infirmity of the manhood. . . . In this one Christ, both appear; The Godhead burst out, as the sun out of a cloud, and shines forth gloriously in miracles, even the raising of the dead, and the humane nature is submitted to contempt and to torment, even to the admitting of death in his owne bosome; . . . but still, both he that raises the dead, and he that dies himself, is one Christ, his is the glory of the Miracles, and the contempt and torment is his too." [71]

Donne thinks that when S. John wrote his Epistle (1 John v. 7, 8) there had already been a schism about the two elements of the nature of Christ, and Donne refers to the ancient heresies about the Person of Jesus Christ against which S. John wrote this Epistle.

"When the Apostle writ this Epistle, it seems there had been a *schisme*, not about the *Mysticall* body of Christ, the Church, but even about the Naturall; that is to say, in the person of Christ there had been a schisme a separation of his two natures: for as we see certainly before the death of this Apostle, that the Heresie of *Ebion*, and of *Cerinthus* (which denied the divine nature of Christ) was set on foot (for against them purposely was the Gospell of Saint John written) so by *Epiphanius* his ranking of the Heresies, as they rose, where he makes *Basilides* his Heresie, (which denied that Christ had any naturall body) to be the *fourth* heresie, and Ebions, to be the *tenth*, it seems that they denied his *humanity* before they denied his Divinity. And

[71] *LXXX Sermons*, 40.

therefore it is well collected, that this Epistle of *St. John,* being written long before his Gospell, was written principally and purposely against the opposers of Christ's humanity, but occasionally also in defence of his divine nature too. Because there is *solutio Jesu,* a dissolving of Jesus, a taking of Jesus in peeces, a dividing of his Natures or of his offices. . . ." [72] Donne believed that the divine and the human were so much a part of the nature of Christ that they were not dissolved even in His descent into hell or in His burial in the grave.[72]

Hooker has briefly and admirably summed up the characteristics of the Person of Christ.

"In four words . . . *truly, perfectly, indivisibly, distinctly;* the first applied to his being God, and the second to his being Man, the third to his being of both One, and the fourth to his still continuing in that one Both; we may fully by way of abridgment compromise whatsoever Antiquity hath at large handled either in declaration of Christian belief, or in refutation of the foresaid heresies." [73]

CHRIST AND THE HOLY GHOST

Donne says that though the Holy Ghost is the third Person in the Trinity it does not mean that the third was created after the second, or is below Him in dignity.

"We use to say, They differ *ordine,* because the Son is the second and the Holy Ghost the third person; but the second was not before the third in time, nor is above him in dignity." [74]

As to the generation of the Holy Ghost, Donne declares that He did not proceed like the Son from the Father alone but from both the Father and the Son, that is why He is called "The Spirit of Gods," *spiritus Elohim.*

"And *De Modo,* for the manner of his proceeding, we need, we can say but this, As the son proceeds *per modum intellectus* (so as the mind of man conceives a thought) so the Holy Ghost proceeds *per modum voluntatis;* when the mind hath produced a thought, that mind and that discourse and ratiocination produce a will; first our understanding is settled, and that understanding leads our will.

[72] *L Sermons,* 6.
[73] *Ecc. Pol.,* Bk. V.
[74] *LXXX Sermons,* 34.

And nearer than this (though God knows this be far off)
we cannot goe, to the proceeding of the Holy Ghost." [75]
Donne says that the Holy Ghost in His person and operation is
really from Christ Himself.[76]

> " The blessed Spirit of God then, the Holy Ghost, the
> third person in the Trinity . . . this Holy Ghost is here
> designed by Christ in his Person, and in his operation."

Donne has discussed the views of S. Basil and S. Augustine
about the Holy Ghost, but he agrees with the latter.

> " Now in what sense is the Holy Ghost said to have
> come in the name of Christ ? " [76]

S. Basil interpreted the coming of the Holy Ghost in the name
of Christ by pointing out that one principal name of Christ is
verbum, the word, which is also the name of the Holy Ghost;
and as the Son manifested the Father, the Holy Ghost mani-
fests the Son.   Donne says:

> " S. Augustine gives another sense. . . . The Holy Ghost
> is the union of the Father and the Son.   As the body is not
> the man, nor the soul is not the man, but the union of the
> soul and body, by those spirits, through which the soul
> exercises her faculties in the organs of the body, makes up
> the man ; so the union of the Father and Son to one
> another, and of both to us, by the Holy Ghost, makes up the
> body of the Christian Religion."

As Christ came to " collect and to govern " the Church, the
Holy Ghost comes so that " salvation may be appropriated to
particular soules by way of application." [77]

According to Donne there have been three advents of
Christ ; an advent of Humiliation, an advent of Glory and an
advent of Grace, which is symbolized by the Holy Ghost.

> " We use to note three Advents, three comings of Christ.
> An Advent of Humiliation, when he came in the flesh ; an
> Advent of Glory, when he shall come to judgement ; and
> between these an Advent of Grace, in his gracious working
> in us, in this life ; and this middlemost Advent of Christ is
> the Advent of the Holy Ghost . . . when Christ works in us,
> the Holy Ghost comes to us." [78]

Donne says that the Father is a Propitious Person, the Son is

[75] *LXXX Sermons,* 34.
[76] *LXXX Sermons,* 28.
[77] *Ibid.*
[78] *LXXX Sermons,* 36.

F

a Meritorious Person, and the Holy Ghost is a Familiar Person, because through the Grace of Christ He can always be near us.

> "The Father came near me, when he breathed the breath of life into me, and gave me my flesh. The Son came near me, when he took my flesh upon him, and laid downe his life for me. The Holy Ghost is alwaies neare me, alwaies with me . . . if I doe but open my heart to myself, I may see the Holy Ghost there, and in him, all that the Father hath Thought and Decreed, all that the Son hath said and done, and suffered for the whole world, made mine." [79]

Thus to Donne the assurance of salvation is the "internal operation of the Holy Ghost," [80] and therefore it is the mediation of "this Blessed Person of the glorious Trinity " [79] which gives to the human soul that sense of holy cheerfulness which is the mark of a true Christian.

CHRIST AND THE VIRGIN MARY

Donne had written his "Litany" in 1609, in which he had addressed the following lines to the Virgin Mary:

> "For that faire blessed Mother-maid,
> Whose flesh redeem'd us; That she—Cherubin,
> Which unlock'd Paradise, and made
> One claime for innocence, and disseiz'd sinne,
> Whose wombe was a strange heav'n for there
> God cloath'd himself, and grew,
> Our zealous thankes wee poure."

Edmund Gosse commenting on this declared:

> "From a dogmatic point of view it shows Donne still imperfectly divorced from the tenets of Rome. He still proclaims the efficacy of the Virgin Mary's prayers to God the Father for souls on earth." [81]

But the invocation of the Virgin Mary does not mean that Donne believed in the Roman Catholic view of the position of the Virgin Mary as embodied in the Roman Breviary (approved at the Council of Trent), which says:

[79] *LXXX Sermons*, 28.
[80] *XXVI Sermons*, 20.
[81] Gosse, Vol. I, p. 265.

"Hail, O Queen, Mother of Mercy Hail,
Our life, our sweetness, our hope!
To thee we fly, the banished sons of Eve."

The fundamental position of the Protestant Churches was that they insisted that the salvation could be attained through faith in Christ alone, and though they accepted His birth of a pure Virgin, and the honour due to the Virgin Mary as the Mother of God, they held that the soul should come to Christ direct without the intercession of the Virgin Mary or the Saints.

Donne rejected the Roman Catholic view that the Virgin Mary had any definite part in our Redemption, as Eve had in our Fall.

"But, God forbid any should say, that the Virgin *Mary* concurred to our good, so, as *Eve* did to our ruine . . . it cannot be said . . . that by one woman innocence entered, and life: The Virgin *Mary* had not the same interest in our salvation, as *Eve* had in our destruction: nothing that she did entered into that treasure, that ransom that redeem'd us." [82]

Speaking of the Roman Catholic invocation of the Virgin Mary, Donne said:

"They that call upon the Bishop of Rome, in that voyce, *Impera Regibus,* command Kings and Emperours admit of that voyce, *Impera filio,* to her, that she should command her Sonne." [83]

He, however, denied the contention of the Anabaptists that Christ was not of the same substance as His Mother, for "had it not been so, Christ had not beene true Man, and then, Man were yet unredeemed." [83] Christ is her Son, but the Virgin Mary had no part in the Redemptive Mission of Christ.

"His setling of Religion, his governing the Church, his dispensing of his graces, is not by warrant from her." [84]

She was thus blessed amongst women (as the Angel said to her, "Blessed art thou amongst women"), above women, but "not above any person of the Trinity." [84]

[82] *XXVI Sermons*, 24.
[83] *LXXX Sermons*, 2.
[84] *Ibid.*

THE RESURRECTION

We shall consider briefly Donne's views on the Resurrection under the following five sub-divisions :

    (1) The Resurrection of Christ, His Ascension, and His descent into Hell.

    (2) Heresies about Christ's Resurrection.

    (3) The Resurrection of the Christians.

    (4) The Relation of the Body and Soul in Resurrection.

    (5) Proof of our Resurrection.

The Resurrection of Christ and our Resurrection

The Resurrection of Christ is the theme to which Donne recurs again and again in his divine poems as well as in his sermons, for it signified to him the triumph of the Son of Man on death with all its horrors of bodily disintegration and its message of final extinction.

In his sonnet of the Resurrection Donne says :

> " And life, by this death abled, shall controule
> Death, whom thy death Slue ; nor shall to mee
> Fear of first or last death, bring miserie,
> If in thy little booke my name thou enroule,
> Flesh in that long sleep is not putrified,
> But made that there, of which, and for which 'twas ;
> Nor can by other meanes be glorified."

Donne says that our resurrection will be like the Resurrection of Christ, though not in the same manner for the Transfiguration of Christ is the only example of the Resurrection we have. He says that Christ's Transfiguration is the only " patterne, which hath been given us of that glory, upon earth, which is the Transfiguration of Christ ; for that Transfiguration of his, was a representation of a glorified body in a glorified state . . . the Transfiguration of Christ, is the best glasse to see this resurrection, and state of glory in." [85]

Donne points out that we should not entangle ourselves " in the intricacies, and subtilties of the Schoole " [85] in determining " how was that transfiguration wrought ? " but we should content ourselves by saying that " Christ had still the same true, and reall body, in itself." [85] The Transfiguration did not change Christ's body, but He could not be easily recognized due to the celestial glory encircling His face.

" It gave him not another face, but it super-immitted such a light, such an illustration upon him as by that irradiation, that coruscation, the beames of their eyes were scattered, and disgrated, dissipated, so, as that they could not collect them, as at other times, nor constantly, and confidently discern him." [86]
It was why Peter, James and John, who saw the Transfigured Christ, recognized Him, and therefore we, after our resurrection in Heaven, shall also be easily known and recognized.

" When Christ was transfigured in the presence of Peter, James, and John, yet they knew him to be Christ." [87]
Transfiguration did not change Him, nor shall glorification so change us, as that we shall not be known. In the case of the Apostles who saw Christ here in the glorified state, Donne argues, that either God " abated the light of glory," which has no proportion to the capacity of mortal men, or He exalted their " sense of seeing supernaturally," but in Heaven we shall not see by the light of Nature but in the light of glory, which is proper to that state.

Donne, however, points out that the Resurrection of Christ, though clearer than our resurrection, was more mysterious, for it was " still a mystery, out of the compasse of reason," [88] and it was different from our resurrection in that He was raised by a divine power inherent in him, while we shall be raised by the Power of God, working from outside us.

" And then, as it was above our reason, so, howsoever it be our proofe, and our patterne for our resurrection, yet it was above our imitation. . . . We shall be raised by a power working upon us, he rose by a power inherent, and resident in himselfe." [88]

As to *Christ's Ascension* Donne says that the words of the Angel that " He is not here, for he is risen " clearly prove that Christ was bodily lifted into Heaven.

" For, if the Angel argue fairely, logically, sincerely

[86] *L Sermons*, 15.
[87] Donne says that Moses had also a proportion of this Transfiguration which Christ received in full measure. " When Moses came down with his shining face, though they were not able to looke long upon him, they knew him to be *Moses* " (*L Sermons*, 15).
[88] *LXXX Sermons*, 21.

(He is not here, for he is risen) then there is no necessity, there is no possibility of this omnipresence, or this multi-presence; for then the Angel's argument might have been denied, and they might have replyed, what though he be risen, he may be here too, for he may be in divers places; But the Angel concludes us in this *for,* he cannot be here, for he is risen; Because he is risen, he can not be here in the sepulchre, so as that you may embalm his body, Because he is ascended, he cannot be here. . . ." [89]

Christ's Descent into Hell

Article III of the Thirty-Nine Articles (1571) " of the going downe of Christe into Hell " affirmed that " As Christe died for us, and was buried : so also it is to be believed that he went downe into hell." The meaning of the words in the Apostles' Creed, " He descended into Hell," gave rise to much discussion in the seventeenth century, largely due to Calvin's interpretation.

The discussion centred round the proposition whether Christ went into Hell " personally and locally " or only virtually, " in power and operation." Donne declared that this Article is one of those mysteries of religion which should be accepted through faith and not be made a subject which could be decided by reason or argument.

" And so also have our times by asking . . . How Christ descended into Hell, produced so many answers, as that some have thought it no Article at all, some have thought that it is all one thing to have descended into hell, and to have ascended into heaven and that it amounts to no more than a departing into the state of the dead. But *servate depositum,* make much of that knowledge which the Holy Ghost hath trusted you withall, and believe the rest." [90]

He held that when Christ descended into Hell His body and soul had parted in death, the divine and human in Him did not part; Christ the Man was dissolved (for the union of the soul and body makes a man) but Christ the Lord Incarnate remained intact, that is the union of the divine and human was not dissolved.

" There was *Solutio Corporis,* Christ's body and soul were parted, but there was no *Solutio Jesus,* the divine

[89] *LXXX Sermons,* 25.
[90] *LXXX Sermons,* 30.

nature parted not from the humane, no not in death, but adhered to, and accompanied the soule, even in hell, and accompanied the body in the grave." [91]

Heresies

Donne says that as there have been more heresies about the humanity of Christ than about His divinity, so there have been more heresies " about the Resurrection of his body, and consequently of ours, than about any other particular Article, that concerns his Humiliation, or Exaltation."

Simon Magus totally denied that there ever was any Resurrection of Christ, and though the Gnostics acknowledged the Resurrection they affirmed that it was of the soul alone and not of the body.

Donne then gives a long catalogue of the heresies connected with the Resurrection; of the *Arabians,* who allowed a temporary death to the soul as well as to the body; of *Eutychius,* who included the body together with the soul in the Resurrection, but so enlarged the qualities of the body that it was no longer a body; of the Armenians, heretics, who declared that we all shall rise in the perfect sex, but none as women; of *Origen,* who allowed the Resurrection of both the body and the soul for a thousand years, and then promised complete annihilation; and of the curious heresy of Hymeneus and Philetus (whom S. Paul mentions) who not only confined Resurrection to the soul but also said that the baptized already had had a Resurrection.[92]

The Relation of the Body and Soul in Resurrection

Donne believed that the immortality of the soul will not be complete without the immortality of the body.

" Nay the immortality of the soule, will not so well lie in proofe, without a resuming the body. For, upon those words of the Apostle, *If there were no Resurrection we were miserablest of all men,* the Schoole reasons reasonably; naturally the soul and body are united; when they are separated by death, it is contrary to nature, which nature

---

[91] *L Sermons.*

[92] Donne says that most of these heresies were based on the misinterpretation of this Scripture that *Flesh and blood cannot inherit the Kingdom of God,* and that those " Fathers who opposed those heresies, so divers from one another, do interpret these words diversly, according to the heresie they opposed " (*L Sermons,* 15).

still affects this union; and consequently the soule is less perfect, for this separation; and it is not likely, that the perfect naturall state of the soule, which is, to be united to the body, should last but three or foure score yeares, and, in most, much less, and the unperfect state, that in the separation, should last eternally, for ever : so that either the body must be believed to live againe or the soule believed to die." [93]

He says that the soul and body are independent, and that the soul cannot do anything without the help of the body.

"All that the soule does, it does in, and with, and by the body. 'And therefore . . . the body is washed in baptisme, but it is that the soul might be made cleane . . . The body is signed with the crosse, that the soul might be armed against tentations; And againe . . . my body received the body of Christ that my soule might partake of his merits. . . . These two, Body and Soule, can not be separated for ever, which, whilst they are together concure in all that either of them doe. . . ." [93]

Donne rejects the view of Damascenus that there could be no Resurrection of the Soul, for it is immortal, and that if we could prove that there be any Resurrection, necessarily it would be of the body.

"Take Damascene's owne definition of Resurrection. . . . A Resurrection is a second rising to that state, from which anything is formerly fallen. Now though by death, the soul do not fall into any such state, as that it can complaine (for what can that lack, which God fils?) yet by death the soule falls from that, for which it was infused, and poured into man at first, that is, to be the forme of that body, the King of that Kingdome; and therefore, when in the generall Resurrection, the soule returnes to that state, for which it was created, and to which it hath had an affection, and a desire, even in the fulnesse of the joys of Heaven, then when the soule returnes to her office, to make up the man (because the whole man hath body as well as the soul) therefore the soule hath a Resurrection; not from death, but from a deprivation of her former state; that state which she was made for, and is ever inclined to." [94]

Donne believed that Image of God was also in the body as well

[93] *LXXX Sermons,* 18.
[94] *LXXX Sermons,* 19.

as in the soul.[95]   The Christian conception of Resurrection is bound up with the immortality of the body.

> " The soul of man is not safer wrapt up in the bosom of God, than the body of man is wrapt up in the Contract, and in the eternal Decree of the Resurrection." [96]

He imagines Resurrection as a state in which the body shall retain all its proper form and features.

> " In the same body, and the same soul, shall be recompact again, and be identically, numerically, and individually the same man.   The same integrity of body and soul, and the same integrity in the organs of my body, and in the faculties of the soul too." [97]

All the bodies in Resurrection will be of the same age, for there will be no Time at the Day of Judgment.   Donne says that as two men of equal age, if one slept while the other kept awake, will be of the same age in the morning, so that those who had been lying in the grave for many ages, and those who would die at the Last Day, shall enter into their bodies together at the same time.[98]

> " No antiquity, no seniority for their bodies; neither can their souls who went before be said to have been there a minute before ours, because we shall all be in a place that reckons not by minutes." [99]

The Proof of the Resurrection

Donne says that the Resurrection can be proved by reason, for " the Holy Ghost himself sends us to Reason, and to the *Creature,* for the doctrine of the Resurrection." [100]   Donne points out that everything in Nature has a Resurrection, and will man, the noblest of all creatures, be denied the Resurrection?

> " Doe all kinds of earth regenerate, and shall onely the churchyard degenerate?   Is there a yearely Resurrection of every other thing, and never of men? . . . All things are preserved, and continued by dying. . . . And canst thou,

---

[95] *L Sermons,* 29.   He says, "None of these ways, not because God hath a body, not because God assumed a body, not because it was intended that Christ should be born, before it was intended that man should be made, is this Image of God in the body of man."

[96] *XXVI Sermons,* 21.

[97] *L Sermons.*

[98] *XXVI Sermons,* 21.

[99] *Ibid.*

[100] *L Sermons,* 14.

O man, suspect of thyself, that the end of thy dying is an
end of thee." [100]

But the surety of our Resurrection is not in the phenomena
of Nature but in Christ Himself " who is already crown'd,
with that Resurrection." [101]

There are several passages in Donne's sermons, where his
discourse on the Resurrection of the body rises to that sombre
majesty which characterizes his meditations on death.

" Propose this body to thy consideration in the highest
exaltation thereof, as it is the *Temple of the Holy Ghost*.
Nay, not in a metaphor, or comparison of a Temple, or any
other similitudinary thing, but as it was really and truly the
body of God, in the person of Christ, and yet this body
must wither, must decay, must languish, must perish. When
Goliah had armed and fortified this body, And Jezabel had
painted and perfumed this body, And *Dives* had pampered
and larded this body, as God said to *Ezekiel* when he
brought him to the *dry bones, Fili hominis, Sonne of Man,
doest thou thinke these bones can live?* They said in their
hearts to all the world, can these bodies die? And they
are dead. *Jezabel's* dust is not Amber, nor Goliah's dust
Terra sigillata, Medicinall; nor does the serpent, whose
meat they are both, finde any better relish in *Dives* dust,
than in *Lazarus*. . . . That nothing in temporall thing is
permanent, as we have illustrated that, by the decay of that
which is God's noblest piece in Nature, the body of man;
so we shall also conclude that, with this goodnesse of God,
that for all this dissolution and putrefaction, he affords this
body a Resurrection." [102]

ANGELS

According to Donne, we can know the nature of God better
than the nature of the Angels, for God has manifested Himself in creation while our knowledge of the nature of the
Angels is merely abstract.

" We have better means to know the nature of God,
than of Angels, because God hath appeared and manifested
himself more in actions than Angels have done." [103]

[101] *L Sermons*, 11.
[102] *LXXX Sermons*, 80.
[103] *XXVI Sermons*, 25.

He says that our knowledge is confined to the fact that we do not know the nature of Angels.

"Now when we would tell you, what those *Angels* of God in heaven, to which we are compared, are, we can come no nearer telling you that, than by telling you, we can not tell." [104]

He says that (a) they are creatures, (b) that they are spirits, and (c) that their office is to execute God's will upon men.

" We know they are *spirits* in *Nature*, but what the nature of a spirit is, we know not; we know they are Angels in *office*, appointed to execute God's will upon us; but, *How* a spirit should execute those bodily actions, that *Angels*, doe, in their owne motion, and in the transportation of other things, we know not : we know they are *creatures*; but whether created with this world (as all our later men incline to think), or long before (as all the *Greeke*, and some of the *Latin* fathers thought) we know not." [104]

And though they are classed with the other creatures of God, time has no effect on them as on other things.

" They are creatures *made* yet not a minute *elder now*, than when they were first made, if they were made before all measure of time began." [104]

As to their number and faculties, Donne points out there has never been any agreement either among the ancient Fathers or in the Reformed Churches.

" We know that for their number, and for their faculties also, there may be one *Angel* for every man; but whether there be so, or no, because not onely amongst the Fathers, but even in the Reformed Churches, in both sub-divisions, *Lutheran*, and *Calvinist*, great men deny it; and as great affirme it, we know not." [105]

We have also no knowledge of the manner in which Angels apprehend and understand things.

"We know the Angels know, they understand, but whether by that way, which we call in the Schoole, *cognitionem matutinam*, by seeing all in God, or by a

---

[104] *L Sermons*, 1.

[105] *L Sermons*, 1. In another sermon he declared that nobody can ever tell the number of Angels " he created *Angels*; How many, how great? Arithmetique lacks *numbers* to express them, proportion lacks dimensions to figure them " (*L Sermons*, 32).

clearer manifestation of the *species* of things to them than to us, we know not." [106]

Donne says that Angels are divided into various orders, but their number is not definitely known. Dionysius the Aeropagite had divided them into nine orders, but S. Gregory and S. Bernard differ from him, while Athanasius considers that there are more than nine orders; [107] Donne says it is enough to declare, like S. Augustine, " that there are distinct orders of Angels, assuredly I believe, but what they are, I can not tell." [107]

However Donne has summed up his own conception of Angels more in a poetic rather than in the scholastic manner.

" They are *primogeniti Dei,* God's eldest Sonnes; They are super-elementary meteors, they hang between the nature of God, and the nature of man, and are of middle condition; And (if, we may offencelessly express it so) they are *enigmata divina,* The Riddles of Heaven, and the per-plexities of speculation. But this is but till the Resurrec-tion; Then we shall be like them, and know them by assimilation." [107]

[106] Robert Boyle also says that the better understanding and knowledge of Angels is due to their nearness to God, the source of all knowledge. " Besides, those happy spirits, of whom Scripture tells us that they *stand before God,* and that they *continually see his face,* have by that privilege the blessed opportunities of discovering in the Deity they contemplate and serve many excellencies, which even they could never but by experience have formed any thoughts of " (*Works,* Vol. I, p. 295).
[107] *L Sermons,* 1.

CHAPTER IV

THE first beginning of the speculation on the nature of
" Fall " and " original sin " is to be found in the different
views taken as to the origin of the human soul. The Eastern
Fathers and Jerome and Hilary in the West held that God
created each soul out of nothing and then joined it to a body
derived from its parents. According to this theory, which is
called " creationism," original sin would lie in the body and
not in the soul. The speculations of the Western Fathers
and Gregory of Nyssa in the East led them to the view that
the human soul was derived from its parents. Thus all mankind sinned " in Adam." With Origen in the East and
Tertullian in the West, the two classical types of the Fall
doctrine begin to distinguish themselves. Origen in his
Alexandrine period elaborated the theory of a pre-natal "Fall"
of individual souls borrowed from Plato's " Phædrus."
" Original Righteousness " is thus affirmed, but referred to a
transcendental mode of existence, whilst " original sin "
becomes a weakness rather than a disease, a *privatio* rather
than a *depravatio*. In his later period at Cæsarea, he took
a more pessimistic view of human nature and held that a
" sense of guilt " is inherent in the conception of " original
sin." The fundamental element in Tertullian's elaboration of
the " Fall " doctrine is the belief in the corporeity of the human
soul, which is based on the theory of the " seminal identity."
Thus according to Tertullian *" vitium originis "* affects all
those who are born of the common stock. He strongly asserts
that " original sin " is a positive corruption and not a mere
infirmity. But we must remember that the early Fathers, like
Justin Martyr and Clement of Alexandria, took an optimistic
view of human nature. They held that the " Fall " deprived
man of his supernatural bias towards righteousness, but left
him a fundamentally sound nature. Thus " original sin "
was taken to mean a loss of higher goodness, a *" privatio
naturæ."* This mild conception of original sin in the Early

Church was mainly due to the great prominence then given to the doctrine of the Logos, to the contemplation of Christ, as the Wisdom and Reason of the Father.[1]   This aspect of Christ, which was elaborated by the Early Fathers with the help of the Platonic doctrine of a Logos also strengthened their controversial position against the Gnostics who claimed that they had achieved inward illumination through their philosophy.   But S. Augustine took a gloomier view of the " Fall " and its consequences, and maintained that man's original bias towards righteousness was natural to him, therefore man in losing the supernatural gifts which Adam had possessed before the " Fall " really fell below the level of his true nature and thus the " Fall " has resulted in the entire corruption of human nature.   S. Augustine says :

> " God indeed created man upright, being himself the author of natures, not of vices.   But man, having of his own free-will become depraved, and having been justly condemned, begat a posterity in the same state of depravation and condemnation.   For we all were in that one man (Adam), seeing that we all *were* that one man who fell into sin through the woman, who was made of him before the sin.   Not yet had we received those individually created and distinct shapes, in which we were as separate individuals to live ; but there was a seminal nature, from which we were to be propagated ; and, this having been vitiated by sin, tied with the chain of death, and justly condemned, it follows that man would be born from man in no other condition ' than that in which Adam was after the Fall.' " [2]

Thus man inherits a nature which is corrupted at the root, and has a positive inclination towards evil—it is not a mere " *privatio naturæ*," but " *depravatio naturæ*."   This doctrine of the " Fall " of S. Augustine was fully developed during his famous controversy with Pelagius.   Pelagius denied that the " Fall " has resulted in the corruption of human nature at all. He taught that the " Fall " had injured nobody but Adam, and the widespread existence of sin was due to the following

---

[1] J. B. Mozley, *Augustinian Doctrine of Predestination*, Chap. IV.
[2] For a detailed account of the Augustinian doctrine and its influence in the West, see *The Ideas of the Fall and of Original Sin*, by N. P. Williams, Chapters V and VI.

of Adam's bad example.[3]   He held that infant baptism confers positive graces, but not "remission of sins," as infants have no sins or sinfulness to be remitted.   He was even prepared to allow that some men before Christ had lived free from sin.[3]

At the Reformation the controversy about the "Fall" and original sin was again revived.   The Early Church had on the whole taken a mild view of the "Fall" and its effects.   The Council of Trent only referred to "the loss of holiness and righteousness"; it affirmed the reality of the Free-will, denied that concupiscence was in any real sense sin, and declared that Baptism does really efface the taint of original sin.   On the other hand, both Calvin and Luther agreed with S. Augustine in maintaining that the Fall has resulted in the total depravity of human nature, in emphasizing the sense of guilt in original sin and in holding the doctrine of irresistible grace.   They both, however, unlike S. Augustine, taught that some men were predestined to evil.   They main- tained that the supposed "good deeds" of the Pagans and Jews were really sins, for according to the doctrine of "total depravity" all the acts of unregenerate men were necessarily sinful.[4]   The Apology for the Confession of Augsburg laid down that "it is both false and an insult to Christ to assert that men do not sin when they fulfil the Commandments of God, apart from Grace."   This view is based upon the favourite text of S. Augustine in the Epistle to the Romans (Rom. xiv. 23).

THE ANGLICAN VIEW OF THE FALL AND
ORIGINAL SIN

I

The Anglican view of the Fall and original sin is embodied in Article IX "of original sin," Article X "of Free-will" and Article XIII "of works before justification."   The Ninth Article adopts a mediating position.   It follows S. Augustine when it speaks of "the fault and corruption (*depravatio*) of the nature of everyman, that naturally is engendered by the offspring of Adam, whereby man is very far gone from original righteousness, and is of his own nature inclined to

---

[3] He was offended by the Prayer of S. Augustine " Give me the power to do what thou commandest and then command what thou wilt."   " Give the power," he cried, " why you have the power " (Williams, Chapter V).
[4] Calvin, *Instit. Christ. rel.*, ii, 3 ;   Williams, p. 430.

evil." It, however, carefully avoids the Calvinistic view of
"total depravity." The latter part of the Article which deals
with concupiscence is also vague.

> "And, although there is no condemnation for them that
> believe and are baptized, yet the Apostle [5] doth confess, that
> Concupiscence and lust hath of itself the nature of sin."

It does not say that it is truly and properly sin. The Calvinists
held that concupiscence was sin. The Council of Trent said
that it was not "truly and properly sin but . . . is of sin
and inclines to sin."

II

It is against the background of these theological discussions
that Donne's attitude towards the doctrine of the "Fall" and
original sin becomes intelligible. He believed in the terrible
reality of original sin as the consequence of the "Fall." He
rejected Pelagianism and, following S. Augustine, held that
as all mankind was "in Adam" we all concurred in Adam's
sin.

> "That all being derived from Adam, Adam's sin is
> dérived upon all. Onely that one man that was not
> naturally deduced from Adam, Christ Jesus, was guilty of
> no sin,[6] . . . and though this original sin that overflowes
> us all, may in some sense be called . . . a sin without an
> elicite act of the Will (for so it must needs be in children)
> and so properly no sin, yet as all our other faculties were . . .
> in *Adam,* and we sinned wilfully when he did so, and so
> originall sin is a Voluntary Sin." [7]

Donne does not think that original sin consists in following
Adam's bad example; he argues that an involuntary act
cannot be a sinful act, but our wills which were "in Adam"

---

[5] The Apostle is probably S. Paul, reference being to "Rom. vii. 17 as
expounded by S. Augustine," Kidd, *Thirty-nine Articles,* p. 127.

[6] Donne elsewhere explaining the sinlessness of Christ said that "In
the Schoole very many and very great men, have thought and taught
that the humane nature of Christ, though united Hypostatically to the
Divine Nature, was not merely by that Union impeccable, but might have
sinned, if besides that Union, God had not infused, and super-infused
other graces, of which other graces, the Beatificall Vision, the present
sight of the face and Essence of God, was one. Because (say they) Christ
had from his conception, in his Humane Nature, that Beatificall Vision
of God, which we shall have in the State of Glory, therefore he could
not sin. . . . This Beatificall Vision, this sight of God was the cause, or
seal, or consummation of Christ's Perfection, and impeccability in his
Humane Nature" (*LXXX Sermons,* 17).

[7] *LXXX Sermons,* 37.

concurred in sinning with Adam as they do in committing any actual sin in life. Donne, like S. Augustine, attaches a sense of " guilt " to " original sin."

" For though St. Augustine confesse, that there are many things concurring *originall* sin, of which he is utterly ignorant, yet of this he would have no man ignorant that to the *guiltinesse* of originall sin, our own Wills concurre as well as to any actual sin. An involuntary act, can not be a sinfull act; and though our Will work not now, in the admitting of original sin, which enters with our soule in our conception, or in our inanimation and quickening, yet, at first . . . as every man was in *Adam,* so every faculty of every man, and consequently the Will of every man concurred to that sin, which therefore lies upon every man now : so that that debt, originall sin, is as much *thine* as *his.*" [8]

Donne has discussed the problem of the " infusion of the original sin " in the soul in a subtle way. He held that there was no interval between the " creating " of the soul and its " infusion " into the body.

" As St. Augustine cannot conceive any interim, any distance, between the creating of the soul, and the infusion of the Soul into the body, but eases himself upon that *Creando infundit,* and *infundendo creat,* The creation is the infusion and the infusion is the creation, so we can not conceive any Interim, any distance, between the infusing and the sickning, betweene the coming and the sinning of the Soule." [9]

In another sermon he argues that there could be no sin in the *soul* itself, for it would mean that God created something that was *evil,* nor was there sin in the *substance* of which Man was made, for God would never infuse soul into an evil substance.

" There was no sinne in that substance of which we were made; for there had been sin in that *substance,* that substance might be damn'd, though God should never infuse a soul into it; and *that* cannot be said well then; God whose

[8] *L Sermons,* 21 ; also see *LXXX Sermons,* 32, where Donne quotes S. Augustine to the effect that as " the whole nature of every particular man was in Adam, so also were the faculties, and so the will of every particular man in him."
[9] *LXXX Sermons,* 51.

goodnesse, and wisdome will have that substance to become a Man, he creates a *soul for it,* or creates a soul *in it* . . . here is no sin in that soul that God creates; for there God should create something that were *evill;* and cannot be said." [10]

Donne therefore concludes that there is " no sin in the *body alone;* None from the soul, no sin in the *soul alone ";* but the very minute that the union of the body and soul takes place (which makes a man) original sin enters into us.

" In the first minute that my soul is infused the Image of God is imprinted in my soul; so forward is God in my behalf, and early does he visit me. But yet *originall sin* is there as soon as that Image of God is there. My soul is capable of God, as soon as it is capable of sin . . . and the Image of God, and the Image of *Adam,* originall sin, enter into me at once, in one, and the same act." [11]

Donne considers " original sin " the " root of sin," [12] and though sanctifying grace communicated through baptism abolishes the guilt of original sin, it leaves concupiscence still in existence.[13]

" And truly, if at this time, God would vouchsafe mee my choice, whether hee should pardon mee all those actuall and habituall sins, which I have committed in my life, or extinguish originall sinne in me, I should chuse to be delivered from originall sin, because though I be delivered from the *imputation* thereof by Baptism, so that I shall not fall under a Condemnation for originall sin onely, yet it remains in me, and practises upon me, and occasions all the other sins that I commit. [14]

He here again adopts the Augustinian position that baptism annuls the *reatus* of concupiscence but leaves *actus* still in existence.[15]

[10] *L Sermons,* 19. Donne thus here seems to reject Origen's theory of a " pre-natal fall," according to which we were really fallen spirits who fell in another world. See Williams, pp. 212–18.

[11] *L Sermons,* 19.

[12] *L Sermons,* 22.

[13] Donne says " Our concupiscencies dwell in us, and prescribe in us, and will grow upon us as wormes, till they deliver our bodies to the wormes of the grave, and our consciences to the worme that never dyes " (*LXXX Sermons,* 51).

[14] *L Sermons,* 22.

[15] Williams, p. 367. This is the view of S. Thomas Aquinas also; see *ibid.,* p. 403.

Donne is however careful to point out that though our will concurred in sinning with Adam, it has still the power to avoid positive sin, and that we sin out of our own choice and not through any necessity of sinning imposed upon us by God.

" And for the other debts, which grow out of this debt (meaning ' original sin '), for *actuall sins*, they are thine, out of thine own choice; Thou mightest have left them undone, and wouldest needs doe them; for God never induces any man into a perplexity, that is, into a necessity of doing any particular sin." [16]

In another sermon Donne declared that as God was supreme Goodness and had no room for " evil " in Himself, He could no more make man sin than sin Himself.

" Not good only so, as that he hath no roome for ill in himself, but good so too, as that he hath no room for any ill will towards any man; no man's damnation, no man's sin, growes radically from this tree.   When God had made all, sayes Tertullian, he blessed all . . . God could no more meane ill, than doe ill; God could no more make me sin, then sin himself." [17]

Donne held that there is no " ill purpose " in God that compels us to commit sin, and that Christ's mercy and grace were available equally to all.

" Our destruction is from our owne sin, and the Devill

[16] *L Sermons*, 21.

[17] *LXXX Sermons*, 17. Donne here seems to differ from S. Augustine, for according to Mozley, S. Augustine " explained the corruption of human nature to mean the loss of free-will; and this statement was the fundamental barrier which divided the later from the earlier scheme and *rationale* of original sin. The will, according to the earlier school, was not substantially affected by the fall. . . . But in Augustine's scheme the will itself was disabled at the fall, and not only certain impulses to it withdrawn, its power of choice was gone, and man was unable not only to rise above a defective goodness, but to avoid positive sin. He was thenceforth, prior to the operation of grace, in a state of necessity on the side of evil, a slave to the devil and to his own inordinate lusts " (*Augustinian Doctrine*, pp. 125, 126).   How far this representation of S. Augustine's doctrines of original sin, Nature and Grace is true, I am not competent to judge. S. Thomas Aquinas, however, denied that Free-will was destroyed by the Fall. (See *Summa Theologica*, Part I, qu. 83, Art. 1 (of Free-will) where he says, " Man has free-will: otherwise counsels, exhortations, commands, prohibitions, rewards and punishments would be in vain . . . he acts from free judgment, and retains the power of being inclined to various things. . . . And for as much is it necessary that man has a free-will, as he is rational.")

that infuses it, not from God, or any ill purpose in him that enforces us. The blood of Christ was shed for all that will apply it, And the Holy Ghost is willing to fall, with the sprinkling of that blood, upon all that do not resist him." [18] The original sin has left an inherent tendency towards sin in Man, but Man has the freedom of choice not to sin. Donne has illustrated this idea in a poetic way.

" No man can assign a reason in the sun, why his body casts a shadow : why all the place round about him, is illumin'd by the sun, the reason is in the sun ; but of his shadow, there is no other reason, but the grosness of his owne body : why there is any beam of light, any spark of life, in my soul, he that is the Lord of light and life, and would not have me die in darkness, is the onely cause ; but of the shadow of death, wherein I sit, there is no cause, but mine own Corruption.[19]   And this is the cause why I do sin ; but why I should sin, there is none at all." [20]

S. Augustine had condemned unbaptized infants to eternal punishment though of the " mildest kind," [21] for though they had committed no actual sin, they were equally tainted with original sin which involves guilt and therefore deserves punishment.   S. Thomas Aquinas rejected this severe view of the lack of Baptism in infants and therefore held that the unbaptized children went to *limbus puerorum,* where they would not behold God. He conceived original sin as the lack of original righteousness, the loss of which will result in the loss of the Beatific Vision in the next life. As the infants had never received through baptism the capacity for the Beatific Vision, they would not feel its loss, and so their state will be one of natural happiness.[22]

Donne did not share the belief that unbaptized infants were condemned to Hell,[23] and he objected to the conception of *Limbo* as a place of happiness and rest, for there could be no

---

[18] *LXXX Sermons,* 33.
[19] Donne is here referring to the fact that Adam brought death on himself and consequently on mankind through the Fall. He said in another sermon, " Adam was made to enjoy an immortality in his body ; He induced death upon himselfe. . . . God did not induce death, death was not in his purpose " (see *LXXX Sermons,* 19).
[20] *XXVI Sermons,* 7.
[21] Williams, p. 327.
[22] Williams, p. 406.
[23] *L Sermons,* 7.

greater "torment" in the next life than the loss of the Beatific Vision.

"*Blessed are the pure in heart,* sayes Christ, *for they shall see God.* If they should not see God, they were not blessed. And therefore they who place children that die unbaptized, in a roome, where though they feel no torment, yet they shall never see God, durst never call that roome a part of heaven, but of hell rather; though there be no torment yet, if they see not God, it is hell." [24]

DONNE'S CONCEPTION OF SIN

Donne had an acute consciousness of sin to which he gave an intense expression in his divine poems as well as sermons. The "inner-Conflicts of his tormented" [25] soul heightened his sense of sin; and we do not find in his devotional poetry either the serene joy of the Illuminated Soul or the ardour and tenderness of the mystic's love for God, but, as Professor Grierson says, an "effort to realize the majesty of God, the heinousness of sin, the terrors of Hell, the mercy of Christ." [26]

This aspect of Donne's poetry has been admirably discussed by his various critics. [27] But it is in his sermons that Donne discourses on sin from the dogmatic and philosophical point of view, and it is here that we find that his passionate belief in the mercy of Christ and goodness of God was as strong as his realization of the terrible reality of sin.

Though Donne defines sin at various places as a disorder, [28] as a violation of the Law of God, [29] as a deformity, he treats it primarily in its relation to God. Like S. Augustine (in opposition to the Manichæans), Donne emphasized the voluntary nature of sin. He repudiated Manichæism which conceived Evil as a distinct and co-eternal principle in antagonism with the good. [30]

[24] *LXXX Sermons,* 17.
[25] H. J. C. Grierson, *The Poems of John Donne,* Oxford, 1933. Introduction, p. xiv.
[26] Grierson, Vol. II, Introduction, p. li.
[27] By Mrs. Evelyn Simpson in her *Study of the Prose Works of John Donne;* see Chapters II, V; H. I'A. Fausset, *Donne, A Study in Discord,* who has over-emphasized Donne's sense of sin and discord; J. B. Leishman, *The Metaphysical Poets.*
[28] *LXXX Sermons,* 37.
[29] *Ibid.,* 58.
[30] In S. Augustine's twenty-three books, *Contra Faustum Manichæum,* Faustus, the great teacher of Manichæism, is represented as admitting his belief only in two principles and not in two gods.

Donne held that "nothing is Essentially good, but God, ... Essentiall goodness in God himselfe ... that this Essentiall goodness of God is so diffusive, so spreading, as that there is nothing in the world, That doth not participate of that goodnesse."[31] He is, however, careful to point out that there is no goodness in the world apart from God, and that there is nothing so good in itself that it can subsist without its utter dependence on God, the source of all goodness.

"For, when it is ordinarily inquired in the Schoole whether anything be essentially good, it is safely answered there, that if by essentially we mean independently, so good as that it can subsist of itself, without dependance upon, or relation to any other thing, so there is nothing essentially good : But if by essentially, we mean that whose essence and being is good, so everything is essentially good." [32]

He further points out that the error of the Manichæans arose from their refusal to recognize that evil could not issue from God, who was all goodness.

"For we see the Manichees, and the Marcionites and such other Heretiques in the Primitive Church, would rather admit and constitute two Gods, a good God, and a bad God, then be drawn to think, that he that was the good God, indeed, could produce any ill of himselfe or meane any ill to any man, that had done none." [32]

Donne quotes the arguments of S. Augustine to prove that there is nothing naturally evil.

"But it is strongly argued by S. Augustin, If there be anything naturally evil, it must necessarily be contrary to that which is naturally good; and that is God. Now *Contraria aqualia,* saies he, whatsoever things are contrary to one another, are equal to one another, so if we make anything naturally evill, we shall slide into the Manichees error, to make an Evill God. . . . To say that anything is naturally evil is an heresie." [33]

Donne says that Christians should learn from Plato not to exaggerate the power of evil and sin in the world, when compared to the all-embracing goodness of God.

"*Plato* says *creavit quia bonus,* therefore did God create

[31] *LXXX Sermons,* 17.
[32] *Ibid.*
[33] Donne is here quoting Anselm : *Haereticum esse dicere Malum esse aliquid.*

us, that he might be good to us, and then he adds *Bono
nunquam inest invidia,* certainly that God, that made us out
of his goodnesse, does not now envy us that goodness which
he hath communicated to us; Certainly he does not wish us
worse, that so he might more justly damne us, and therefore compell us by any positive decree, to sin, to justify his
desire of damning us: Much lesse did this good God hate
us, or meane ill to us, before he made us, and made us onely
therefore, that he might have glory in our destruction.
There is nothing good but God, there is nothing but goodnesse in God." [34]

Donne while preserving the freedom of the human will, also
rejected the doctrine of Pelagius that sin consists of individual
actions only, that our will and nature are not affected by the
" Fall," that infants are born without any taint of original sin,
and that man could perform good works without the help of
the divine grace.[35]

DONNE AND THE SCHOLASTIC CONCEPTION OF
SIN AS A PRIVATION

Donne has discussed the conception of sin as a *Privation*
in several of his sermons.[36] Mrs. Evelyn Simpson has mis-
represented Donne's notion of evil and sin as a privation, for
she has taken " negation " and " privation " to mean the
same thing.[37] She says:

" The insistence of the mystics on the immanence of God
has led certain of them to consider evil as mere negation.
. . . Thus Gregory of Nyssa says: ' There is nothing
which falls outside of the Divine nature, except moral evil
alone. And this, we may say paradoxically, has its being in
not being.' For the genesis of moral evil is simply the
privation of being. Donne adopts this view in *The Litanie.*
As sinne is nothing, let it nowhere be—and later puts it
forward tentatively in some of his sermons."

The quotation from Gregory of Nyssa does not support

[34] *LXXX Sermons,* 17.
[35] See Chapter V for a full discussion of the relation of Nature and
Grace.
[36] See *LXXX Sermons,* 17; *L Sermons,* 21; *L Sermons,* 20; *LXXX
Sermons,* 35.
[37] *A Study of the Prose Works of John Donne,* by E. M. Simpson; see
the chapter " The Mediæval and Mystical Elements in Donne's
Thought," pp. 107–10.

Mrs. Simpson's statement that mystics consider evil as "mere negation," for Gregory is only referring to evil as "the *privation* of being."

This distinction between "negation" and "privation" is implied in Donne's discussion of the nature of sin and evil.

"We must not think to ease ourselves in that subtilty of the Schoole, *Peccatum nihil;* That sin is nothing, because sinne had no creation, sin hath no reality, sin is but a deflection from, but a privation of the rectitude required in our actions . . . ill things are no things, ill, considered as ill, is nothing; for, whatsoever is anything, was made by God, and ill, sin, is no creature of his making. This is true; but that will not ease my soul, no more then it will ease my body, that *Sicknesse* is nothing and *death* is nothing: for, death hath no reality, no creation, death is but a privation; and *damnation,* as it is the everlasting losse of the sight and presence of God, is but a privation. And therefore as we fear death, and fear damnation, though in discourse, and in disputation, we can make a Schoolshift, to call them *nothing,* and but privations, so let us fear sin too, for all this imaginary *nothingnesse,* which the heat of the School hath smoak'd it withall. Sin is so far from being nothing, as that there is nothing else but sin in us." [38]

Donne while affirming that the Scholastic doctrine of sin as a *privation* is true (for "sin is no creature of his [God's] making") makes it clear that this notion of sin does not in any way lessen the terrible reality of sin. [39] He is in fact here following S. Thomas Aquinas in emphasizing the distinction between *negation* and *privation.* Defining the nature of evil, S. Thomas wrote:

"The perfection of the Universe requires that there should be inequality in things, so that every grade of goodness may be filled up. Now, one grade of goodness is that of the good which cannot fail. Another grade of goodness

[38] *L Sermons,* 21.

[39] Donne presumed that his audience knew the true significance of the scholastic conception of sin, for he confidently declared, "You know, I presume, in what sense we say in the Schoole, *Malum nihil,* and *Peccatum nihil,* that evil is nothing, sin is nothing" (*LXXX Sermons,* 17). Mrs. Simpson's remark that "This view of sin, however, often conflicts with the Christians' strong moral sense" is based on a misunderstanding of the Scholastic doctrine of sin.

is that of the good which can fail in goodness, and this grade is to be found in existence itself ; for some things there are which cannot lose their existence as incorruptible things, while some there are which can lose it, as things corruptible . . . Now it is in this that evil consists, namely, in the fact that a thing fails in goodness. Hence it is clear that evil is found in things, as corruption is found ; for corruption is itself an evil." [40]

Having explained the presence of evil, S. Thomas points out that evil is not a *pure negation,* but a *privation.*

" Evil is distant from simple being and from simple *not being,* because it is neither a habit *nor a pure negation, but a privation."* [41]

Donne, following S. Augustine, defines sin as a violation of the eternal law ;[42] therefore sin signifies disorder and as there is nothing but order and harmony in God, God cannot be the author of sin.

" There is no order in the Author of sin, and therefore the God of order can not, directly or indirectly, positively or consecutively, be the Author of sin.   There is no order in sin itselfe.   The nature, the definition of sin, is disorder, *Dictum, factum, concupitum contra legem* (St. Augustine); God hath ordered a law, and sin is an act; if we cannot do that, it is a word ; if we dare not do that, it is a desire against that law." [42]

Donne declared that the definition of sin as a violation of the eternal law also implies that it is an aversion from the end which God has proposed for Man.

" So that our affecting of anything, as our end, which God hath not proposed for our end ; or our affecting of

---

[40] *Sum. Theol.,* Part I, qu. 48, Art. 2.

[41] *Ibid.,* this is in reply to objection 1, " It seems that evil is not found in things. For whatever is found in things is either something, or a privation of something, that is *not being.* But Dionysius says (*Div. Nom.,* IV) that evil is distant from existence, and even more distant from non-existence.   Therefore evil is not at all found in things."

[42] *LXXX Sermons,* 37. S. Thomas Aquinas also defines sin as " Contrary to the eternal law."   " Now there are two rules of the human will : one is proximate and homogeneous, viz. the human reason ; the other is the first rule, viz. the eternal law, which is God's reason, so to speak. Accordingly Augustine includes two things in the definition of sin ; one pertaining to the substance of a human act, which is the matter, so to speak, of sin, when he says, *word, deed,* or *desire ;* the other, pertaining to the nature of evil, which is the form, as it were, of sin, when he says, " *Contrary to the eternal law.*"   The *Sum. Theol.,* II, qu. 71.

true ends, by any other wayes then he hath proposed, this is a disordering of God's providence, as much as we can, and so a sin." [43]

He seems to be closely following S. Thomas here, who says:
"The eternal law first and foremost directs man to his end, and in consequence, makes man to be well disposed in regard to things which are directed to the end: hence when he (St. Augustine) says, *Contrary to the eternal law,* he includes aversion from the end and all other forms of inordinateness." [44]

S. Thomas held that "sin is not a pure privation but an act deprived of its due order, hence sins differ specifically according to the objects of their acts rather than according to their opposites . . ." [45]

Donne also emphasized that sin is not only a privation, it is also an "action deprived of that rectitude which it should have."

"Sin is not therefore so absolutely nothing, as that it is (in no consideration) other than a privation, onely *Absentia recti* and nothing at all in itselfe: but, not to enter farther into that inextricable point, we rest in this, that sin is *Actus inordinatus,* It is not only an obliquity, a privation, but it is an action deprived of that rectitude which it should have; It does not onely want that rectitude, but it should have that rectitude, and therefore hath a sinful want." [46]

I think that Donne realized the terrible reality of sin not only through his own personal experience, but also through his meditations on the Passion of Christ;[47] that the Son of God had to be sacrificed to atone for the sins of mankind shows the awful power of sin.

"We shall not dare to call sin merely, absolutely nothing, if we consider either the punishment due to sin, or the pardon of that punishment, or the price of that pardon . . . That which God could not pardon in the way of justice without satisfaction, that for which nothing could be a satisfaction, but the life of all men, or of one man

[43] *LXXX Sermons,* 37.
[44] *Sum. Theol.,* II, II, qu. 71.
[45] *Ibid.,* II, II, qu. 72.
[46] *LXXX Sermons,* 35.
[47] He once said "The whole life of Christ was a continuall passion; others die Martyrs, but Christ was born a Martyr" (*LXXX Sermons,* 4).

worth all, the Sonne of God . . . that which could change
the frame of Nature in Miracles, and the God of Nature in
becoming Man, that that deserved that punishment, that
that needed that ransome (say the Schoolmen what they
will of privations) can not be meerely, absolutely nothing,
but the greatest thing that can be conceived, and yet that
shall be forgiven." [48]
Donne agreed with S. Augustine in declaring that there were
three ways to escape sin.   The first being :
  " *occasionis substractione;* that's the safest way, not to
  come within distance of a tentation ; secondly, *resistendi
  data virtute.*   That the love and the fear of God imprinted
  in him, made him strong enough for the sin."
The third was attained through the Contemplation of God :
  " *affectionis sanitate;* that his affections, had, by a good
  diet, by a continuall feeding upon the contemplation of
  God, such a degree of health and good temper, as that some
  sins he did naturally detest, and though he had not wanted
  opportunity, and had wanted particular grace, yet he had
  been safe enough from them." [49]
Donne held that the purity of thought and the absence of
a " sinful delight " in our past sins was necessary to attain
the peace of conscience.[50]   He once called every sin an
" incision of the soule, a letting of the foule blood " and
delight in sin " going with open veines into a warm bath." [51]
It was essential for the purification of the self that the heart
and mind should be free of attachment to anything that does
not lead to God.   The cleansing of conscience was therefore
as important as living a pure life.
  " If S. *Paul's* case were so far thy case as thou wert in
righteousness unblameable, no man, no woman able to
testifie against thee, yet when the records of all thoughts
shall be laid open, and a retired and obscure man shall
appear to have been as ambitious in his cloister as a
pretending man at the Court, and a retired woman in her
chamber, appear to be as licentious as a prostitute woman
in the stews, when the heart shall be laid open, and this

[48] *LXXX Sermons,* 35.
[49] *L Sermons,* 10.
[50] *LXXX Sermons,* 56.
[51] *Ibid.,* 13.

laid open too, that some sins of the heart are the greatest
sins of all (as Infidelity, the greatest sin of all, is rooted in
the heart) . . . our own consciences shall be our execu-
tioners and precipitate us into that condemnation." [52]
Donne in discussing the attitude of the Anglican Church
towards "Contrition," "Confession" and "Satisfaction"
declared that "All these (howsoever our Adversaries slander
us, with a Doctrine of ease and a Religion of liberty) we
require with more exactnesse, and severity, then they doe."

Contrition

He wrote, "for Contrition, we doe not, we dare not say,
as some of them, That Attrition is sufficient; that it is
sufficient to have such a sorrow for sin, as a naturall sense,
and fear of torment doth imprint in us, without any motion
of the fear of God : we know no measure of sorrow great
enough for the violating of the infinite Majesty of God, by
our transgression."

Confession

Donne held that the Anglican Church does not deny a
"necessity to confesse to man" but that "we require a particular detestation of that sin which we confesse, which they
require not."

Satisfaction

As for satisfaction he agrees with the rule of S. Bernard,
"Condigna satisfactio malè facta corrigere, our best satisfaction is to be better in the amendment of our lives : And
dispositions to particular sins, we correct in our bodies by
Discipline, and Mortifications; And we teach, that no man
hath done truly that part of Repentance, which he is bound
to doe, if he has not given Satisfaction, that is, Restitution, to
every person damnified by him." [53]

Donne, while recognizing the need of private devotion,
insisted that the remission of sin could only be obtained
through the means ordained by the Church.

"Let no Soule say, she can have all this (assurance of
Pardon) at God's hands immediately, and never trouble the
Church. That she can passe her pardon between God and
her, without all these formalities, by a secret repentance.

[52] *LXXX Sermons,* 14.
[53] *LXXX Sermons,* 56.

It is true, beloved, a true repentance is never frustrate
. . . Though thou be a Church in thy fancy, if thou have
no more seales of Grace, no more absolution of sin, then
thou canst give thyself, thou wilt perish. . . . Thou maist
be a sacrifice in thy chamber, but God receives a sacrifice
more cheerfully at Church . . . only the Church hath the
nature of a Surety." [54]

It is only in the Ordinances of the Church that " there is
an Infallibility of *Remission* upon true repentance, and in a
Contempt or neglect of which ordinances, all Repentance is
illusory, and all Remission but imaginary." [55]   He held that
true repentance results in possessing a personal testimony of
the forgiveness of sin ;[56] when God sends the Holy Ghost " as
the spirit of consolation to blow away all scruples, all diffi-
dences, and to establish an assurance in the Conscience." [57]
Donne seems to have attained the peace of conscience, for he
speaks with great sincerity and conviction of having received
a personal testimony of the pardon of his sins of youth.[58]
Donne was never anxious to gloss over the sins of his past life.
He freely acknowledged them to his audiences, " Let all the
world know all the sins of my youth, and of mine age too,
and I would not doubt, but God should receive more glory
and the world more benefit, then if I had never sinned." [59]

He calls himself as one " that is rectified, refreshed, restored,
re-established by the seales of God's Pardon." [59]   But the
supreme testimony of our reconciliation to God consists in the
" Union with God," which he defines as " the peace of conscience, the undoubting trust and assurance of salvation " in
this life, and the possession of the " Beatific Vision " in the
next, for " there is nothing good in this life, nothing in the
next, without God, that is, without sight and fruition of the
face and presence of God." [60]

---

[54] *LXXX Sermons,* 37 ; also see *L Sermons,* 27.
[55] *LXXX Sermons,* 28.   For Donne's arguments against Indulgences,
see *LXXX* Sermons, 54.
[56] *L Sermons,* 9.
[57] *LXXX Sermons,* 56.
[58] *Ibid.*
[59] *Ibid.,* 13.
[60] *Ibid.,* 17.

CHAPTER V

JOHN DONNE AND SOTERIOLOGY

DONNE's treatment of the three elements of soteriology:
(1) The Atonement
(2) Justification and
(3) Predestination

has an important bearing on his position as a theologian, for the doctrines of Predestination and Justification by faith were the two most controversial and difficult problems of Protestant theology in the seventeenth century.

The doctrines of Salvation, Justification, Free-will and Predestination assume a significant importance in western theology with the famous controversy of the British monk Pelagius with S. Augustine. Three great Schools within the Catholic Church interpreted these doctrines in their own different ways. To the Nominalists the human will was the determining factor, the Augustinians mainly relied on grace, while S. Thomas tried to strike a balance between these two.

Luther by his nature and personal experience was inclined to the Augustinian doctrines; the belief that grace is the sole means of salvation, and that we are the passive agents of the Divine Will, and that the taint of original sin is so strong in us that we are powerless to do good, strongly appealed to the pessimistic temperament of Luther. Though Luther acquired the terminology of the Augustinian theologians, he differed consciously from S. Augustine in essential and important points.[1]

It was during the years 1513—1516, when he was lecturing on the Psalms and the Epistle to the Romans, that Luther

---

[1] Luther wrote to John Brenz (May, 1531) that "Personally I quote Augustine as completely on our side on account of public opinion with regard to him although he gives an inadequate account of Justification by faith. Believe me, my dear Brenz, the controversy concerning the justice of faith is complicated and obscure. You will realize it, if you turn your eyes away completely from the law, and fix your mind firmly on the 'gratuitous promise.' So as to grasp that it is by the promise and through Christ that we are justified and pleasing in the sight of God and so find peace. . . ."

began to formulate his theory about Justification by faith alone. He was preoccupied with the problem of the certainty of salvation and the part that Man's work can play in it in relation to the Divine Will. He was acutely conscious of the conflict of the flesh and spirit within the human soul, of the contrast between the ideals we try to achieve and the poverty of our achievement.

In his *Commentary on the Psalms* (1514) he wrote :

" Man realizes that he is frail and of no account, when he tries to do what he can in the conviction that he can because he knows how. The passion of anger, pride, lechery is considered easy to overcome, from afar off and by people without experience. But near at hand, it is found to be extremely difficult, *nay insurmountable: Such is the teaching of experience.*"

The paradox which confronted Luther was that while he believed that the sinner could be justified by fulfilling the Law, he also held that the fulfilment of the Law was beyond the power of the sinner, as he had no free-will, and was dependent on the workings of the Divine Spirit.

When Luther was lecturing on the Epistle to the Romans, he realized that he had discovered the solution to the above paradox. Though man alone is quite incapable of fulfilling the Law, he does it through Christ. God redeems us through Christ, and thus imputes His justice to us ; Justification is therefore wholly by faith alone in this sense that we are saved through the merits of Christ and not by our own works. The Redemption has been brought about by the Sacrifice and Blood of Christ ; and the promise of Redemption is the essence of the Gospel. If we have implicit faith in this promise, salvation is ours. This Lutheran elaboration of the doctrine of Salvation is called the dogma of Justification by faith without works.[2]

In estimating the main spirit of the Elizabethan Articles

---

[2] Luther had developed this dogma as early as 1515, but about this time curiously enough he also maintained that no one could be sure of salvation, and he objected to Indulgences on the same principle that they gave a false sense of security to the erring soul. It was in 1518 that he came to the conclusion that the possession of a sense of the certitude of salvation was essential, for it was bound up with our implicit faith in the redemptive mission of Jesus Christ. Luther maintained this doctrine of salvation in his debate with the Legate Cajetan at Augsburg, and fully described it in his *Commentary on the Epistle to the Galatians* (1519).

we should remember that they were considerably influenced by the " Augsburg Confession." The Articles tenth and eleventh and twelfth on " Free-will " and " Justification " and " Good Works " respectively were adapted from it.[3] Article XI " of Justification of man " is essentially Lutheran in its conception.

" We are accompted righteous before God, only for the merite of our Lord, and Saviour Jesus Christe, by faith and not for our owne workes or deservynges. Wherefore, that we are justified by fayth onely, is a most wholesome doctrine, and very full of comfort, as more largely is expressed in The Homilie of Justification."

Though Donne believed that faith was necessary for salvation, he does not seem to hold the doctrine that righteousness could only be achieved through " faith and not for our owne workes or deservynges." Donne argues that neither faith nor works alone could be the *cause* of our salvation ; they are interdependent, and that God alone is the cause of our Justification.[4] This line of argument was also adopted by other Anglican theologians like George Bull and John Selden.

" For, in the first place, since justification is the act of God alone, and produced entirely without us, how our faith or any actions of ours can give any physical assistance in effecting our justification, is altogether inconceivable. And, in the next place, every instrumental cause, as we have already hinted, operates according to its own peculiar nature, and the production of the effect may be properly attributed to it. Now, since justification is entirely the gracious act of God, by which he pardons our sins and grants us salvation, it is extremely absurd to say, that either our faith or our work, or anything else of ours, forgives our sins, or makes us acceptable. Which, however, is said

[3] The other Articles derived from the Augsburg confession (1551) are the second dealing with the eternal generation and consubstantiality of the Son, the third entitled " of the Holy Spirit " ; and the list of the books which are to be regarded as belonging to the Sacred Canon (which forms an appendix to the sixth Article) has also been copied from the same confession ; see Hardwick, *A History of the Articles of Religion,* pp. 123–6.

[4] He says : " Those questions are not so impertinent, but they are in a great measure unnecessary, which are moved about the cause of our righteousnesse, our justification . . . let us be content that God is the cause, and seek no other " (*LXXX Sermons,* 37).

by those who call faith the instrumental cause of justification." [5]

Donne, explaining the significance of the word " cause " in
relation to justification, said :

" We must never slacken that protestation, that good
works are no cause of our justification. But we must
alwaies keep up a right signification of that word, Cause,
for Faith itselfe is no cause; no such cause, as that I can
merit Heaven by faith. . . . If it were possible to believe
aright, and yet live ill, my faith should doe me no good.
. . . Faith is but one of those things, which in several
senses are said to justifie us. It is truly said of God, *Deus
solus justificat,* God alone justifies us, . . . nothing can
effect it, nothing can worke towards it, but onely the meere
goodnesse of God."

Donne declared that in a sense Christ alone justifies us because
through His obedience to the will of God, He became the
instrument of the goodness of God.

" As the efficient justification, the gracious purpose of
God had done us no good, without the materiall satisfaction, the death of Christ had followed; And as that
materiall satisfaction, the death of Christ would do me no
good, without the instrumentall justification, the apprehension by faith; so neither would this profit without the
declatory justification, by which all is pleaded and established. God enters not into our material justification, that
is onely Christs; Christ enters not in our instrumentall
justification, that is onely faiths. Faith enters not in our
declaratory justification (for faith is secret) and declaration
belongs to workes. Neither of these can be said to justify
us alone, so, as that we may take the chaine in pieces, and
thinke to be justified by any one link thereof; by God
without Christ, by Christ without faith, or by faith without
works; And yet every one of these justifies us alone, so, as
that none of the rest enter into that way and that meanes,
by which any of these are said to justifie us." [6]

In another sermon Donne declared that " Now this judging
according to works, excludes not the heart, nor the heart of

[5] See George Bull, *Harmonia Apostolica,* translated by Thomas
Wilkinson (1801).
[6] *LXXX Sermons,* 37.

H

the heart, the soule of the soule, Faith." [7]   But this goodness
of the heart must be testified by the deed.

  " The testimony of the heart is in the hand, the testimony
  of faith is in works . . . God judges according to the
  worke, that is, root, and fruit, faith, and work." [7]
Donne thought that though "faith is somewhat a deeper
dye, and tincture, than any works," [8] our works are more
ours than our faith.

  " Our good works are more ours, than our faith is ours.
  Our Faith is ours as we have received it, our work is ours,
  as we have done it . . . to assent or to dissent is our owne,
  we may choose which we will doe. . . . But though this
  faculty be ours, it is ours, but because God hath imprinted
  it in us. So that still to will, as well as to doe, to believe,
  as well as to work, is all from God, but they are from God
  in a diverse manner, and a diverse respect, and certainly
  our works are more ours than our faith is, and man concurres otherwise in the acting and perpetration of a good
  work than he doth in the reception and admission of
  faith." [9]

DONNE AND THE ROMAN CATHOLIC VIEW OF JUSTIFICATION

  The Council of Trent had considered the position of the
Roman Catholic Church towards the doctrine of Justification
in forty-four particular and sixty-one general congregations,
and the final draft of the decree drawn by Cardinals Cervini
and Seripando was approved on January 13th, 1547. It
categorically rejected Luther's doctrine of Justification by
faith alone. It upheld the Catholic doctrine that a measure
of Free-will cannot be denied to Man. Luther had declared
in his book " De Servo Arbitrio " (" On the Bondage of the
Will ") (1525):

  " Free-will is a divine attribute and therefore properly
  applicable only to the divine Majesty. . . . To attribute
  it to man is to deify him and no greater sacrilege can be
  committed."
The Council of Trent finally rejected this doctrine of Luther,
and pointed out that it cannot conceive the "original fall" to

[7] *LXXX Sermons*, 39.
[8] *Ibid.*, 11.
[9] *Ibid.*, 8.

be so absolute as to make Man only a passive agent unable to
co-operate with Divine grace in the work of redemption, and
that Baptism to a certain degree does really remove the taint
of original sin. It rejected Pelagianism and declared that we
could not perform " good works " without the help of grace,
but Free-will has not been destroyed by the " Fall," and Man
remains a moral creature.

> " If any one declares that man's free-will, inspired and
> excited by God, in no way co-operates in response to the
> summons and excitation from God, so preparing to obtain
> the grace of Justification, and that man cannot refuse his
> consent, if he so desires, but that his behaviour is that of an
> inanimate object, that he is in no respect an agent and
> remains for ever passive . . . if any one declares that
> man's free-will has been lost and extinguished since the sin
> of Adam, that it is a purely nominal reality, or rather
> nominal without reality, a fiction introduced into the
> Church by Satan, let him be anathema." [10]

Luther had taught that faith is produced as a divine gift and
that the Redemptive mission of Christ requires no co-opera-
tion of the human will which has become impotent through
original sin. Donne believed in free-will, though he recognized that it required divine grace to strengthen it. Donne,
following S. Thomas, pointed out the difference between the
" instinct " of the brute animals, and " the faculty of will "
in man. He compares the possession of " Will " in man to
" instinct " in other creatures.

> " So this is God's administration in the Creature, that he
> hath imprinted in them an Instinct, and so he hath some-
> thing to preserve in them : In Man his administration is
> this, that he hath imprinted in him a faculty of will, and
> election ; and so hath something to reward in him. That
> instinct in the Creature God leaves to the naturall working
> thereof in itselfe. But the free-will of Man God visits, and
> assists with his grace to doe supernaturall things. When
> the Creature does an extra-ordinary action above the
> nature thereof (as, when *Balams Asse* spake), the Creature
> exercises no faculty, no will in itselfe ; but God forced it to
> that it did. When Man does anything conducing to super-

[10] Canons 4 and 5 of the Decrees on Justification of the Sixth Session,
13th January, 1547.

naturall ends, though the worke be God's, the will of Man is not merely passive." [11]

In another sermon Donne went so far as to assert that without the Presence of Free-will in Man the grace of God cannot work.

" In the *Application* of that great worke, the Redemption of mankinde, that is, in the conversion of a sinner, and the first act of that conversion, though the grace of God work all, yet there is a *faculty* in Man, a will in Man, which is in no creature but Man, for that Grace of God to worke upon." [12]

He asserted that grace does not destroy the efficacy of " Will " in man, for grace never destroys Nature.

" The will of Man is but God's agent; but still an agent it is: And an agent in another manner, than the tongue of the beast.   For, the will considered, as a will (and grace never destroys nature, nor, though it make a dead will a live will, or an ill will a good will, doth it make the will, no will) might refuse or omit that that it does.   So that because we are created by another Pattern, we are governed by another law, and another providence." [13]

Donne maintained that the grace of God works not independent of will or in spite of it, but through the natural faculties of Man.

" Consider we alwaies the grace of God, to be the sun itself, but the nature of man, and his naturall faculties to be the spheare, in which that sun, that grace moves.   Consider we the Grace of God to be the soule itself, but the naturall faculties of man, to be as a body, which ministers Organs for that Soule, that Grace to worke by. . . ." [14]

Donne, like the Council of Trent, rejected Pelagianism.

[11] *L Sermons*, 29.   S. Thomas gives similar arguments to prove that man possesses Free-will.
" In order to make this evident, we must observe the same things act without judgment, as a stone moves downwards; and in like manner all things which lack knowledge.   And some act from judgment, but not a free judgment; as brute animals.   For the sheep seeing the wolf judges it a thing to be shunned, from a natural and not a free judgment, because it judges, not from reason, but from natural instinct. . . . But man acts from judgment, because by his apprehensive power he judges that something should be avoided or sought."   *Summa Theologica*, Part I, qu. 83.
[12] *L Sermons*, 42.
[13] *L Sermons*, 29.
[14] *LXXX Sermons*, 68.

" To a child rightly disposed in the wombe, God does
give a soule; To a naturall man rightly disposed in his
naturall faculties, God does give Grace. But that soule
was not due to that child, nor that Grace to that man. . . .
Nor so leave all to Grace as that the naturall faculties of man
do not become the servants, and instruments of that Grace.
Let all, that we all seeke, be, who may glorifie God most;
and we shall agree in this, That as the Pelagian wounds the
glory of God deeply, in making naturall faculties Joynt-
commissioners with Grace, so doe they diminish the glory
of God too, if any deny naturall faculties to be the
subordinate servants and instruments of Grace; for as
Grace could not worke upon man to salvation, if man had
not a faculty of will to worke upon, because without that
will man were not man." [15]

Donne points out that salvation is achieved through the will
of man working in complete harmony with the will of God,
and that God does not save any man unless that man wants to
be saved, and is working towards that end.

" So is this salvation wrought in the will, by conforming
this will of man to the will of God, not by extinguishing
the will itselfe, by any force or constraint that God imprints
in it by his Grace; God saves no man without or against
his will." [15]

He laid great stress on the power of " preventing grace " in
saving us from committing those sins which we otherwise
would have done.

" We consider a preventing Grace in God; and that
preventing Grace is before all; for that prevents us so,
as to *visite us when we sit in darknesse.* . . . And when we
call God's Grace by other names than Preventing, whether
Assisting Grace, that it stand by us and sustain us, or
Concomitant Grace, that it work with us, and inanimate
our action, when it is doing, or his *Subsequent* Grace, that
rectifies or corrects an action, when it is done; when all is
done, still it is the *preventing power,* and quality of that
Grace, that did all that in me." [16]

[15] *LXXX Sermons,* 64.
[16] *L Sermons,* 26. While speaking of preventive grace elsewhere, he
declared that " we needed forgiveness, even for the sins which we have
not done. . . . Sayes S. Augustine, I confesse I need thy mercy both for
the sins which I have done, and for those which, if thy grace had not
restrained me, I should have done."

Donne did not believe that we could be saved by faith *alone,* faith and work were interdependent and could not be separated from each other.

"Onely believe, and you shall be saved; And . . . do this, and you shall be saved; As it is truly all one purpose, to say, If you live you may walke, and to say, if you stretch out your legges, you may walke. . . . And therefore, as God gave a Reformation to his Church, in prospering that Doctrine, That justification was by faith onely; So God give an unity to his Church in this Doctrine, That no man is justified that works not; for, without works, how much so ever he magnifie his faith, there is *Dolus in Spiritu, Guile in his spirit.*" [17]

Donne believed that there could be no assurance of salvation without faith, and that it should find concrete expression in works that testify this faith; so far he was in agreement with the Roman Catholic Church.

"This assurance (so far as they will confess it may be had) the Roman Church places in faith, and so far, well; but then, *In fide formata;* and so far well enough too; In those works which declare and testifie that faith." [18]

Donne had said in his "Pseudo-Martyr" that:

"there is more Devotion in our Doctrine of good Works, than in that of the Roman Church, because wee teach as much necessity of them as they doe, and yet tie no reward to them. And we acknowledge that God doth not onely make our faith, to fructifie and produce good Workes as fruits thereof, but sometimes beginnes at our Workes; and in a man's heart morally inclined to doe good doth build up faith. . . ."

But he did not accept the Roman Catholic definition of Works as the Soul, and form of Faith, for "though a good tree cannot be without good fruits, yet it were a strange manner of speech to call that good fruit, the life or the soul, or the form of that tree: so is it, to call works which are the fruits of faith, the life or soul, or form of faith, for that is proper to grace only which infuses faith." [18]

Donne admits that the Roman Catholic Church "acknowledges this neerness of salvation, this assurance in good works;

[17] *LXXX Sermons,* 56.
[18] *XXVI Sermons,* 20.

but say they, man cannot be sure, that their work is good, and therefore they can have no such assurance."

Donne further refers to the view of the Protestant Reformers who believed that there could be no peace of conscience unless we possessed this assurance of salvation.

" They who undertook the reformation of Religion in our Fathers dayes and observing that there was no peace without this assurance, expressed this assurance thus, That when a man is sure that he believes aright, that he hath no scruples of God, no diffidence in God, and uses all endeavours to continue it, and to express it in his life, as long as he continues so, he is sure of salvation, and farther they went not."

Thus the assurance of salvation was a psychological state which rested on an implicit belief in God and as long as it lasted, man had the peace of conscience.

" for when it is said now, now that you are in this state, salvation is near you ; thus much is pugnantly intimated, that if you were not in this state, salvation were further removed from you how so ever you pretend to believe." [19]

But Donne rejected the extreme Protestant view that if you ever once believed in your life you will be saved.[20] Donne recognized the significant fact that it was neither faith nor works which were the " full cause " of our salvation, for it really rested on free Election by God. These were only " mediate causes," faith was " instrumentall," works " declaratory," " faith may be as evidence, works as the seale of it ; but the *cause* is onely the free Election of God. Nor shall we come thither, if we leave out either ; we shall meet as many men in heaven, that have lived without faith, as without works." [21]

The prime cause of our salvation was nothing but the mercy of God. The existence of faith in us " was not the principal and primary cause of his mercy, for the mercy of

[19] *XXVI Sermons,* 20.
[20] Donne said, " And then there arose some, which would reform the Reformers, and refine salvation and bring it into a lesse room ; They would take away the condition, if you hold fast, if you express it ; and so came up roundly and presently to that ; If ever you did believe, if ever you had faith, you are safe for ever, and upon that assurance you may rest."
[21] *L Sermons,* 9.

God is all and above all; it is the effect and is the cause too; there is no cause of his mercy, but his mercy." [22]

PREDESTINATION AND ELECTION

According to Luther all men are so tainted with "original sin," that they deserve eternal damnation, but God out of His free-will selects some who are saved and the rest meet their doom.

He wrote in *On the Bondage of the Will* (1525):

"Through his Will which is immutable, eternal, and indefectible, God foresees, foretells, and realizes all things. This principle is like a lightning flash, blasting and destroy-human freedom absolutely."

But this theory of fatalistic Predestination was fully developed by Calvin. He defined Predestination as "the eternal counsel of God whereby He has determined His Will in respect of every man. *For He did not create them all alike but ordained some to eternal life, the rest to eternal damnation.*"

Calvin gave to this terrible doctrine an austerity so that the people who believed in it rejoiced at the joys of the Elect, and recognized the majesty of Divine justice in condemning others to Hell.

Calvinism was propagated not only by means of books but also by the foundation of a College in 1559 and an academy, and thus Geneva became a centre of Protestant culture.[23] Calvin became the S. Thomas of the Protestant theology and his authority continued to increase so much during the Elizabethan reign that Hooker declared that "the perfectest divines were judged they, which were skilfullest in Calvin's writings." [24]

We are not here concerned with the controversy between Calvinism and High Church Party in the Anglican Church as represented respectively by Dr. Whitaker and Professor Baro, or the formulation of the "Lambeth Articles" which tried to put a Calvinistic interpretation on the Anglican Formularies of Faith,[25] but it should be noticed that the claim of Calvin-

[22] *LXXX Sermons*, 11.
[23] Protestant academies were also founded in France on the Genevan model at Montauban, Sedan, Montpellier and Orange.
[24] Preface to *Eccl. Pol.*
[25] See Strype's *Whitgift*.

istic theologians [26] that their system was derived from S. Augustine helped in no small measure in disarming criticism from laymen and in its wide circulation in England where S. Augustine was held in high esteem.

But the Augustinian doctrine of the Fall and original sin differed, as we have shown, from that of Calvin in important respects in spite of their apparent similarity of language. It is true that S. Augustine, like Calvin, had held that only the Elect were the partakers of the " grace of perseverance," but he had also affirmed that others also were possessed of a true and justifying faith. Calvin, on the other hand, denied the possession of such spiritual gifts to those who were not elected to salvation and thus could not be saved from their ultimate destiny of perdition.[27]

Though Calvinism was strong in England at the time of the formulation of the Elizabethan Articles, in the subsequent revision of the Edwardian Formulary the language of Article XVII on Predestination and Election shows great restraint, and is free from dogmatic assertions. It declared that " Predestination to Life, is the everlasting purpose of God," and that " As the godly consideration of Predestination, and our Election in Christ, is full of sweete, pleasant, and unspeakable comfort to godly persons, and such as feele in themselves the working of the Spirite of Christ . . . because it doth greatly establish and confirme their fayth of eternal salvation to be enjoyed through Christ . . . "

But this Article neither mentions S. Augustine nor Calvin, and points out that the ultimate promise of salvation is contained not in one single doctrine but in the teachings of the Holy Scriptures.

" Furthermore, we must receaue God's promise in such wyse, as they be generally set foorth to us in Holy Scripture : and in our doyngs, that wye of God is to be folowed, which we have expreslye declared unto us in the worde of God."

It was Donne's exalted conception of Divine Mercy and his intense and living faith in the redemptive mission of Christ which instinctively led him to reject the doctrine of Predestina-

---

[26] See Calvin's *Instit. Lib.*, III, c. 22, where he affirmed that he derived the doctrine of Predestination from S. Augustine.
[27] Calvin's *Instit. Lib.*, III, c. 24 and 26.

tion. Donne believed that God's promise of salvation extended to all those who believed in Christ.

" They are too good husbands, and too thrifty of God's grace, too sparing of the Holy Ghost; that restraine God's generall proportions, *venite omnes,* Let all come, and *vult omnes salvos,* God would have all men saved, so particularly, as to say, that when God sayes *All,* he meanes some of all sorts, some Men, some Women, some Jews, some Gentiles, some rich, some poore, but he does not meane, as he seems to say, simply All. Yes; God does meane, simply All, so as that no man can say to another, God meanes not thee, no man can say to himself, God meanes not me." [28]

Donne points out that Christ did not say to the Pharisee that " there is no salvation for thee, thou viper, thou Hypocrite," and that " I have locked iron doore of predestination between salvation and thee." [29] When Christ was asked what a man should do to be sure of salvation, he did not reply that there was no such way, for either you were predestined to salvation or damnation.

" Christ doth not say, there is no such art, no such way, no such assurance here; but you must look into the eternall decree of Election first, and see whether that stand for you or no : But Christ teaches him the true method of this art : for, when he sayes to him, *Why callest thou me good? There is none good but God,* he only directs him in the way to that end, which he did indeed or pretended to seek." [29]

Donne maintains that there is no proof of a rigid doctrine of Predestination in the Holy Scriptures, and that men can only be saved by their faith in Christ.

" So we know his Decree of Election and Reprobation, by the execution; And how is that? Does God ever say, that any shall be saved or damned, without relation, without condition, without doing (in the Old Testament), and in the New Testament, without believing in Christ Jesus? If faith in Christ Jesus be in the execution of the Decree, faith in Christ Jesus was in the Decree itself too." [30]

He points out that our damnation is the result of our own sins, and that the will of God does not determine it in any

[28] *LXXX Sermons,* 33.
[29] *LXXX Sermons,* 17.
[30] *LXXX Sermons,* 33 ; also see *L Sermons,* 35.

respect, for He Himself has tried to purchase our Pardon through the Blood of His own Son.

" Our destruction is from our owne sin, and the Devill that infuses it; not from God, or any ill purpose in him that enforces us. The blood of Christ was shed for all that will apply it, and the Holy Ghost is willing to fall, with the sprinkling of that blood, upon all that do not resist him."

He held that there was an " Antecedent Will " in God and " that Antecedent Will is before all; for by that Will, God would have all men saved." [31]

Donne in an interesting passage quotes S. Augustine as saying that God only predestines to good, and never to evil.

" It is modestly said by S. *Augustine,* and more were immodesty, There is no predestination in God, but to good. And therefore. . . . They are hard words to say, That God predestinated some, not onely *Ad damnationem,* but *Ad causas damnationis,* not only to damnation because they sinned, but to a necessity of sinning, that they might the more justly be damned; And to say, That God rejected some *odio libero,* out of hate, that arose primarily in him- selfe, against those persons, before those persons were created (so much as in God's intentions) and not out of any hate of their sins, which he foresaw." [32]

Donne says that there is no warrant in the New Testament for the conception of a God who would predestine the souls of some men to eternal damnation.

" who lest hee should love man and be reconciled to man hath enwrapped him in an inevitable necessity of sinning, who hath received enough, and enough for that satisfaction of all men, and yet (not in consideration of their future sinnes, but merely because he hated them before they were sinners or before they were anything) hath made it impossible, for the greatest part of men, to have any benefit of that large satisfaction . . . for God hath never said, never done any such thing, as should make us lodge such conceptions of God in ourselves, or lay such imputations upon him." [33]

Donne argues in a subtle way that as the memory of man

[31] *L Sermons,* 26.
[32] *LXXX Sermons,* 33.
[33] *LXXX Sermons,* 69.

cannot extend beyond the Act of Creation (that is the *Time* when God created the World), we can have no knowledge of the decrees of election or predestination, for they are claimed to have been decreed by God eternally.

"First, because the memory can go no farther than the creation; and therefore we have no means to conceive or apprehend anything of God before that. When men therefore speak of decrees of reprobation, decrees of condemnation, before decrees of creation; this is beyond the counsil of the Holy Ghost here . . . for this is to put a preface to Moses his Genesis, not to be content with his *in principio,* to know that *in the beginning God created men and earth,* but we must remember what he did *ante principium,* before any such beginning was."

Donne therefore advises that no one should presume the pardon of his sins because he considers himself to be one of the elect.

"Let no man antedate his Pardon, and say, His sins were forgiven in an Eternall Decree, and that no man that hath his name in the booke of life, hath the addition, sinner, that if he were there from the beginning, from the *beginning* he was no sinner." [34]

He held that the Elect were equally liable to sin and their sins were not judged by God in a different way from those of other men.

"They that are quickened by the Soule of the Soule, Election itselfe, are subject to sin, for all that God sees the sins of the Elect, and sees their sins to be sins . . . we were all dead in *Adam;* and he that is raised againe, even by Election though he be not so married to the world as others are, yet he is as much bound to an obedience to the Will of God declared in his Law, and may no more presume of a liberty of sinning before nor of an impunity of sin after, then he that pretends no such Election, to confide in." [35]

Donne also rejects another sign by which it was claimed that the Elect could be known, their righteousness. He holds that no man can always be sure that he is one of the Elect, for righteousness in us is never constant.

[34] *LXXX Sermons.*
[35] *Ibid.*

" Why, *whom he predestinated, those he called;* and were not they whom he predestinated, and elected to salvation, righteous? Even the Elect themselves have not a constant righteousness in this world : Such a righteousness in this world, as does always denominate them, so, as that they can always say to their own conscience, or so as the Church can always say of them, This is a righteous man : No, nor so, as that God, who looks upon a sinner . . . with the heart and sense of the Church, and speaks of him with the tongue of the Church, can say of him, then, when he is under unrepented sin, This man is righteous : howsoever, if he look upon him, in that Decree which lies in his bosom, and by which he hath infallibly ordained him to salvation, he may say so. No man here, though Elect, hath an equal and constant righteousness; nay, no man hath any such righteousness of his own, as can save him; for howsoever it be made his, by that Application, or Imputation, yet the righteousness that saves him, is the very righteousness of Christ himself." [36]

He believed that there is no *Atonement* but through Christ, and that the knowledge of God alone was not enough for our salvation.

" Knowest thou that there is a God, and that that God created the world? What great knowledge is this? The Jews know it too. . . . It is another Religion, another point of Faith, to know that God had a Son of eternal begetting, and to have a world of late making. God therefore hath shin'd in no man's heart, till he knows the glory of God in the face of Jesus Christ, till he came to the manifestation of God, in the Gospel. So that, that man comes short of this light, that believes in God, in a general, in an incomprehensible power, but not in Christ; and that man goes beyond this light, who will know more of God, than is manifested in the Gospel, which is the face of Christ Jesus; the one comes not to the light, the other goes beyond, and both are in blindness." [37]

Donne has discussed in an interesting manner the scholastic problem whether Christ would have come into the world to

[36] *XXVI Sermons,* 8.
[37] *XXVI Sermons,* 25.

atone for our sins without the Fall of Adam or not.   He explains that there are some who hold that

> " If man had not forfeited his interest and state in heaven by Adam's sin, Christ had not come in the nature of a Redeemer, but . . . out of a brotherly love, and out of a royal favour, to exalt that nature which he did love, and to impart and convey to us a greater and nobler state, than we had in our Creation,"

for it was the purpose of God to dignify the nature of man to the highest degree.   The other view in the School with which Donne seems to agree is that " Christ had not come, if our sins had not occasioned his coming," and this opinion Donne thinks is " more agreeable to the Scriptures, and derives more honour upon God; we cannot err, if we keep with the Scriptures, and in the way that leads to God's glory, and so say with *S. Augustine.* . . . If man could have been saved otherwise, the Son of God had not come in this manner : or if that may be interpreted of his coming to suffer only, we may enlarge it with *Leo.* . . . He who was Creator of the world, had never become a Creature in the world, if our sins had not drawn him to it." [38]   Donne then quotes S. Thomas Aquinas to the effect that

> " God hath appointed all future things to be, but to be so as they are, that is, necessary things necessarily, and contingent things contingently; absolute things absolutely, and conditional things conditionally; He hath decreed my salvation, but that salvation in Christ; He had decreed Christ's coming into this world, but a coming to save sinners.   And therefore it is a frivolous interogatory, a lost question, an impertinent article, to enquire what would have been done if *Adam* had stood." [39]

Donne says that there is no cause of our salvation except the mercy of Christ which is infinite when compared with our faith. [40]

> " My believing that Christ will have mercy upon me, is

[38] *XXVI Sermons,* 14.

[39] *Ibid.*

[40] " When God does work in us, are we saved by that work, as by the cause, when there is another cause of the work itself?   When the ground brings forth good corne, yet that ground becomes not fit for our food. When a man hath brought forth good fruits, yet that man is not thereby made worthy of heaven " (*LXXX Sermons,* 11).

no cause of Christ's mercy; for what proportion hath my
temporary faith with my everlasting salvation. But yet,
though it work not as a cause, though it be not . . . because
he saw it, yet . . . when Christ findes this faith, according
to that gracious covenant, and contract which he hath made
with us, that wheresoever, and whensoever he findes faith,
he will enlarge his mercy finding that in this patient,
he expressed his mercy. . . ." [41]
There is no spiritual security, no salvation, without faith and
the inner working of the grace of God, and all these are
dependent on the infinite Mercy of Christ for the soul of the
sinner.

" Yet grace, if thou repent, thou canst not lacke;
But who shall give thee that grace to beginne?
Oh make thyselfe with holy mourning blacke,
And red with blushing, as thou art with sinne,
Or wash thee in Christ's blood, which hath this might
That being red, it dyes red soules to white." [42]

But disaster awaits those who rely on their own merits for
salvation.

" This security, call it by a worse name, stupidity, is not a
lying down like a Lamb, but a lying down like *Issachers
Asse* between two burdens for two greater burdens can not
be, than sin, and the senselessnesse of sin, . . . what will ye
doe at that day which shall be darknesse and not light? " [43]

For in that darkness it is the glory of God as mirrored in the
face of Christ that alone would save us. The ultimate destiny
of the soul of the Elect is to *die* in Christ, and in doing so be
united to Him.

" I can have no greater argument of thy *mercy* than to
die in *thee,* and by that death, to bee united to him, who
died for me." [44]

---

[41] *LXXX Sermons,* 11.
[42] *Holy Sonnets,* 9.
[43] *LXXX Sermons,* 14.
[44] *Devotions,* p. 41.

CHAPTER VI

JOHN DONNE AND ESCHATOLOGY

Immortality

WE have discussed in detail Donne's conception of the immortality of the soul as well as that of the body in the chapter which deals with " Revealed Theology." To Donne the first attribute of immortality is the eternal life after death.

> " God had been an infinite, a super-infinite, an unimaginable space, millions of millions of unimaginable spaces in heaven, before the Creation. And our afternoon shall be as long as God's forenoon; for, as God never saw beginning, so we shall never see end." [1]

The belief in a future life was commonly held among the Jews long before the coming of Christ; but Donne says it was Christ who for the first time clearly explained the nature of the immortality of the soul as well as of the body, and clearly demonstrated it in His miracles, and in His own Resurrection, and therefore " to dispute against our own Resurrection is seditiously to dispute against the dominion of Jesus; who is not made Lord by the Resurrection, if he have no subjects to follow him in the same way. We believe him to be Lord, therefore let us believe his, and our own Resurrection."

Donne argues that as it was the original intention of God to make both the soul and the body immortal in Heaven, and man only brought death (and divorce between the soul and body) on himself through the Fall, this divorce cannot last after death.

> " As farre as man is immortal, man is a married man still, still in possession of a soule and a body too; And man is for-ever immortall in both; Immortall in his soule by Preservation and immortall in his body by Reparation in the Resurrection." [2]

In another sermon, he has explained the meaning of the soul being immortal through Preservation.

> " And for the Immortality of the soule, it is saflier said

XXVI Sermons, 21.
[2] *LXXX Sermons,* 80.

to be immortall by preservation, than immortall by nature;
That God keepes it from dying, than that it cannot dye." [3]
He says that the resurrection of the body has been made an
article of the Creed because its immortality, like that of the
soul, cannot be proved through reason.

" There are so many evidences of the immortality of the
soule, even to a naturall man's reason, that it required not
an Article of the Creed to fix this notion of the Immortality
of the soule. But the Resurrection of the *Body* is discernible
by no other light, but that of Faith, nor could be fixed by
any lesse assurance than an *Article* of the Creed." [4]
Donne therefore concludes that God created man out of
nothing, and that He shall reintegrate the body after its
dissolution.

" Thinke thyself nothing . . . even that nothing is as much
in his power, as the world which he made of nothing;
And as he called thee when thou wast not, as if thou hadst
been, so will he call thee againe, when thou art ignorant of
that being which thou hast in the grave, and give thee
againe thy forme, and glorifie it with a better being." [5]

Heaven

There are several passages of great beauty and splendour in
which Donne has described the joys which await the sanctified
soul in Heaven.

" Beloved, there is nothing so little in heaven, as that we
can expresse it; But if wee could tell you the fulness of a
soul there, what that fulnesse is, the infinitenesse of that glory
there . . . of that happiness there, how long that happinesse
lasts, if we could make you know all this, yet this Better
Resurrection, is a heaping, even of that Fulnesse, and an
enlarging, even of that Infinitenesse, and an extension, even
of that eternity of happinesse." [6]
He thinks that the greatest spiritual joy you can imagine in
this life is the joy of the martyrs, but the joy in Heaven shall
far exceed even the joys of martyrdom.

" If I had all this joy of all these Martyrs, (which would,
no doubt, be such a joy, as would worke a liquefaction, a

[3] *LXXX Sermons,* 27.
[4] *L Sermons,* 1.
[5] *L Sermons,* 14.
[6] *LXXX Sermons,* 22.

I

melting of my bowels) yet I shall have it *abundantius*, a joy more abundant, than even this superlative joy, in the world to come." [7]

Mr. Hugh I'Anson Fausset has called Donne a " materialist " in his description of Heaven, and a " medievalist " in his conception of Hell.[8] And he has quoted a passage from his sermon to show Donne's use of physical imagery in describing Heaven as " A new earth, where all their waters are milk, and all their milk honey; where all their grasse is corn, and all their corn manna." [8] Though Donne sometimes employs physical imagery to describe Heaven, his conception of the state of the soul in those blessed regions is purely spiritual.

To Donne the first and prime attribute of the soul in Heaven is its complete innocence, and the absence in it of any trace of the original or the acquired sin or sinfulness.

" Christ shall bear witness for me, in ascribing his righteousnesse unto me, and in delivering me into his Father's hands, with the same tendernesse, as he delivered up his owne soule, and in making me, who am a great sinner, they who crucified him on earth for me, as innocent and as righteous as his glorious selfe, in the Kingdome of heaven." [9]

He imagines Heaven as a spiritual state in which his soul shall be " united to the Ancient of dayes, to God himselfe, who had no morning, never began." [9] The soul shall see in that state of glory, the Essence of Good, and become united to Him, for as Donne says,

" In heaven, at last, all things should ebbe back into God, as all things flowed from him, at first, and so there should be no other Essence but God, . . . how much more may we conceive an unexpressible association (that's too far off) an assimilation (that's not near enough), an identification (the Schoole would venture to say so) with God in that state of glory." [10]

But the greatest blessing the soul shall possess in Heaven shall be the eternal vision of the transfigured Christ in flesh with " all clouds of sadness remov'd " from his brow.

" We shall see, and see for ever, Christ in that flesh,

[7] *LXXX Sermons*, 7.
[8] John Donne, *A Study in Discord*, p. 292.
[9] *L Sermons*.
[10] *L Sermons*, 29.

which hath done enough for his friends, and is safe enough from his enemies." [11]

Donne, however, did not believe in the degrees of blessedness in Heaven as conceived by the Roman Catholic Church in its canonization of the Saints.

> "The *Romane Church* makes this blessedness, but an under degree, but a kinde of apprentiship," [12]

for after they have beatified a man, that is, declared him " to be blessed in the fruition of God in heaven," they wait till they are convinced that " much profit will rise, by the devotion, and concurrence of men to the worship of that person, then they will proceed to a canonization, and so, he that in his *Novitiat* and years of probation was but blessed Ignatius and blessed Xavier, is lately become Saint *Xavier,* and Saint *Ignatius.*" [13] Thus Donne points out that the Roman Church perverts the right order and method which consists in first coming " to *sanctification* and then to *beatification* " [13] which he respectively calls the life of grace here, and life of glory in Heaven.

But what really that life of glory shall be nobody can tell, for " the least degree of glory that God hath prepared for that body in heaven, I am not able to expresse, not able to conceive." [14]

Hell

To Donne sin was an awful reality, and after the baptism and Christ's redemptive sacrifice on the Cross, it signified the " Fall " from the grace which he has compared to spiritual death.

> " No man falls lower, than he that falls into a course of sin; . . . A fall is a fearfull thing, that needs a raising, a help; but sin is a death that needs a resurrection; and resurrection is as great a work as the very creation itself."

Sin, therefore, could only be pardoned after the transformation of the whole life, by the regeneration and resurrection of the self.

As sin was not a mere deviation from the path of goodness, but a positive fall from grace, so the punishment of sin was an actual and terrible reality which the soul shall experience in Hell.

[11] *XXVI Sermons,* 25. [13] *L Sermons,* 44.
[12] *XXVI Sermons.* [14] *LXXX Sermons,* 22.

Though Donne sometimes seems to have believed in the physical tortures of Hell,[15] as men generally did in the seventeenth century, his main emphasis is on the misery which the soul shall experience in the withdrawal of God eternally from the sight of the damned in Hell. The possibility that God might leave his soul in the company of the other damned souls and " never thinke more of that soule, never have more to doe with it," [16] was the source of great spiritual agony to Donne. The greatest punishment that the soul could experience would be that it shall

> " lie in darknesse, as long as the Lord of light itself, and never sparke of that light reach to my soule . . . what Brimbstone is not Amber, what gnashing is not a comfort, what gnawing of the worme is not a tickling, what torment is not a marriage bed to this damnation, to be secluded, eternally, eternally, eternally from the sight of God? " [16]

The loss of the sight of God is the greatest affliction the human soul can experience because the presence of the image of God in our soul brings us nearer to Him than any other creature, and because He has afforded greater means of salvation to the Christians through the Scriptures, the Church, and the Sacrifice of His Son than to other men.

> " This damnation, which consists in the losse of the sight and presence of God, be heavier to us than others, because God hath so graciously, and so evidently, and so diversely appeared to us . . . we that have seen him in all the parts of this Commission, in his Word, in his Sacraments, and in good example, and not believed, shall be further removed from his sight, in the next world, than they to whom he never appeared in this." [17]

Mr. Fausset has said that Donne's conception of Hell was purely material and medieval, a " stirring of hell-broth," [18] into which the mercy and compassion of God did not enter.

---

[15] *LXXX Sermons,* 76. Speaking of material hell Donne said, " If there be a figure in the names, and words, of *Fire* and *Wormes,* there is an indisputable reality in the sorrow, in the torment, and in the manifoldnesse, and in the weightinesse, and in the everlastingnesse thereof. For in the inchoation of these sorrows, in this life, and in the consumation of them, in the life to come, *The sorrowes of the wicked are many* and *great* and *eternal* " (*LXXX Sermons,* 63).

[16] *LXXX Sermons,* 76.

[17] *Ibid.*

[18] *Donne,* p. 290.

In Donne's mind the corruption of the body in the grave, the " gnawing of the worm " gave an actual and terrible reality to the tortures of Hell, but, as we have shown, to him the greatest punishment of sin in Hell was the eternal withdrawal of God from the sight of the damned. But at the same time he believed that the mercy of God for the soul was so great that He did not keep any of its sins unpardoned till the Day of Judgment.

" For not onely the sin itselfe, but the iniquitie of the sin, is said to be forgiven; God keeps nothing in his minde against the last day." [19]

Mr. Fausset misinterprets Donne when he says that his (Donne's) conception of God's punishment was that of " a malevolent force," of " violent darkness and pain," while Donne definitely rejected the idea that vengeance was one of His attributes.

" This Terriblenesse which we are called upon to professe of God, is a Reverentiall, a Majesticall, not a Tyrannical terriblenesse. And therefore he that conceives a God, that hath made man of flesh and blood, and yet exacts that purity of an Angel in that flesh, a God that would provide himself no better glory than to damne man," [20]

forms a conception of God that has no warrant in the New Testament, for " God hath never said, never done such thing, as should make us lodge such conceptions of God in ourselves, or lay such imputations upon him." [20]

Donne believed that true repentance could never be unsuccessful, and even relapses into former sins were forgiven by God, for

" the merits of Christ are inexhaustible, and the mercies of God in him indefatigable : As God cannot be deceived with a false repentance, so he cannot resist a true, nor be weary of multiplying his mercies in that case." [21]

Of the repented sins, he says, " And then, my heart can not reproach me of repented sin, without reproaching God himself." [22] Donne thinks that if one could imagine a time when mercy was not an attribute of God, he would become an atheist.

[19] *LXXX Sermons*, 58.   [21] *L Sermons*, 38.
[20] *LXXX Sermons*, 69.   [22] *LXXX Sermons*, 13.

" Let the Devill make me so far desperate as to conceive a time when there was no mercy, and he hath made me so far an Atheist, as to conceive a time when there was no God; if I despoile him of his mercy, any one minute and say, now God hath no mercy, for that minute I discontinue his very Godhead, and his being." [23]

If in spite of the infinite mercy of God, the love of Christ, and the means of salvation and repentance embodied in the Church, we commit sins and then leave them unrepented, we deserve the greatest punishment for our sins in Hell, the withdrawal of God, which Donne calls " an everlasting death."

Purgatory

Donne said in *Pseudo-Martyr* that " all discourse of Purgatory seemes to me to bee but the Mythologie of the Romane Church, and a moral application of pious and useful fables." He rejected the doctrine of Purgatory and declared that there is no mention of its existence in the Old Testament, while the New Testament promises an immediate possession of Heaven after death to the souls of good men.

" As in the Old Testament there is no precept, no precedent, no promise for prayer for the Dead, so in the Old Testament, they confesse there was no Purgatory; no such place as could purifie a soule to that cleannesse, as to deliver it up to Heaven." [24]

Donne thinks it was Plato who invented Purgatory, and thus deserves to be called, in the words of Tertullian, a patriarch of heretics.

" But as the first mention of prayer for the dead was in the time of the Maccabees, so much about the same time was the first stone of Purgatory laid; and laid by the hands of *Plato*. . . . But yet *Platoes* invention, or his manner of expressing it, tooke such roote, and such hold, as that *Eusebius,* when he comes to speak of Purgatory, delivers it in the very words of *Plato* and makes Platoes words his words and *Plato* his Patriarch, for the Greeke Church." [24]

[23] *LXXX Sermons,* 2.
[24] *LXXX Sermons,* 77. Donne says that the abuse of Indulgences was the result of the belief in Purgatory, and so " these Indulgences are the children, the generation of that vipers, the salemanders of that fire, Purgatory."

As to Bellarmine's reliance on (1 Cor. xv. 29) for a definite proof of Purgatory, Donne replies that,

" if we take the words as they are, and as the Holy Ghost hath left them to us, we finde no such manifestation of this Doctrine, no such clear light, no such bonfire, no such beacon, no beame at all, no spark of any such fire of Purgatory." [25]

But Donne thinks that in Bellarmine the spirit of the cardinal has not overcome the spirit of a Jesuit, so he quotes Justinian, a man of his own order, who interprets these words to mean bodily afflictions, suffered by living men for the dead.[25] Donne therefore concludes that there is no warrant in the Scriptures for a belief in Purgatory as a " place of torment, from which our prayer here might deliver soules there." [25]

[25] *LXXX Sermons,* 78.

CHAPTER VII

JOHN DONNE AND MYSTICAL THEOLOGY

IT is not my purpose in this chapter to deal in detail with the mystical theology of John Donne, for the contents of mystical theology are doctrinal as well as experimental; it not only records the mystical experience of the soul, but also enunciates the rules for its guidance, which are based on the Scriptures, the lives of the Saints, and the teachings of the Fathers; there is not enough material available for such an exhaustive survey either in his Sermons or other prose-works of John Donne. Mystical theology has been defined as a " Science which treats of acts and experiences or states of the soul which cannot be produced by human effort or industry even with the ordinary aid of Divine grace." [1] It mainly comprises of :

1. Various forms of prayer.
2. Purification.
3. Illumination.
4. The dark night of the Soul and
5. The Mystical Union.

PRAYER

Donne does not deal with the various forms of prayer, their method, or their practical and mystical import.

There are mainly four forms of Prayer, vocal,[2] mental, affective, and Prayer of simplicity. The vocal prayer denotes verbal expression of the internal act which is implied in every prayer.

Mental Prayer is really a form of meditation in which the various faculties of the soul, memory, intellect, imagination and will are concentrated on some principle, truth or fact as

---

[1] *The Catholic Encyclopædia,* Vol. XIV.
[2] This form of prayer was declared to be unnecessary by Wyclifites and the Quietists. The former objected to it because the soul does not require any words to commune with God, the latter regarded language as a hindrance in the attainment of that passive state of the soul, in which alone the soul could pray. There are, however, several examples of such prayer in the Bible; the Prayer of Israelites in captivity (Exod. ii. 23), the Lord's Prayer (S. Matt. vi. 9) and Christ's own prayer after the raising of Lazarus (S. John xi. 41). *Catholic Encyclo.,* Vol. XII.

an expression of Divine Will as a means of training the soul for its ultimate union with God.[3]

Affective Prayer is the result of a careful training in meditation when the soul can easily rest on the contemplation of pious affection as a means of subordinating itself to the Will of God. In affective prayer the soul does not labour to grasp any truth, but the mere recollection alone fills it with the sentiments of faith, hope, charity and moves it to practise these moral virtues. When these affections are further simplified, because less interrupted by reasoning, and are easily and wholly concentrated on the contemplation of God, this form of prayer is called the *Prayer of Simplicity*. Francis de Sales calls it the prayer of simple committal to God in which we are able to subordinate all the faculties of our soul to the Will and Purpose of God as a means of union with Him. It is through the prayer of simplicity that the soul is trained for its ultimate union with God.

In Donne we do not find any systematic treatment of these various forms of Prayer, but he was fully conscious of the importance of prayer in the devotional life of the Church, and his main interest seems to have been to emphasize the need of Public Prayer, and the necessity of a careful training in private prayer, which he believed could not be attained by every member of the congregation.

Donne has several passages in his sermons where he shows great insight into the Psychology of Prayer. Describing the lack of concentration in private prayer he wrote,

" I lock my doore to myself, and I throw myselfe downe in the presence of my God. I devest myselfe of all worldly thoughts, and I bend all my powers, and faculties upon God, as I think, and suddenly I finde myselfe scattered, melted, fallen into vaine thoughts, into no thoughts, I am upon my knees, and I talke, and think nothing ; I depehend myself in it, and I goe about to mend it, I gather new forces, new

[3] The monastic rules generally prescribed time for common prayer, but it was not till the beginning of the twelfth century that the Carthusians laid down definite times for mental prayer. The Dominicans of Milan in the early sixteenth century had half an hour set apart for mental prayer, every morning and evening, the Franciscans introduced it about the middle of the sixteenth century, but there is no record of methodical mental prayer among the Carmelites until S. Teresa introduced it for two hours daily.

purposes to try againe, and doe better, and I do the same
thing againe. I believe in the *Holy Ghost* but doe not finde
him, if I seeke him onely in private prayer."
It is only in the Church that every individual receives the
spiritual assistance of the Communion of the Saints, and the
Ordinances of the Church.

"But in *Ecclesia,* when I goe to meet him in the *Church,*
when I seeke him where hee hath promised to be found,
when I seek him in the execution of that commission . . . in
his ordinances, and meanes of Salvation of his Church,
instantly the favour of this Myrrhe is exalted, and multi-
plied to me; not a dew, but a flowre is poured out upon
me, and presently followes. . . . The communion of Saints,
the assistance of Militant and Triumphant Church in my
behalfe." [4]

Donne was against "sudden, extemporall inconsiderate" [5]
prayers, and he knew that private prayers were of this nature.

"In sudden and unpremeditate prayer I am not always
I; and when I am not myself, my prayer is not my prayer.
Passions and affections sometimes, sometimes bodily infirmities, and sometimes a vain desire of being eloquent in
prayer, aliens me, withdraws me from myself, and then
that prayer is not my prayer." [6]

Donne says that the Anglican Church in providing set
prayers for the use in churches has followed the example of
the Primitive Church.

"In that African Councell, in which S. *Augustine* was
present the abuse of various formes of Prayers, which divers
churches assumed, it was decreed that no prayers should be
received in the Church, but such as were composed or
approved by the Councell. We have proceeded so too; No
prayers received for publique use, but those that are
delivered by publique authority." [7]

He declared that "The Church of God by his ordinance,
hath set his stampe upon a liturgie and service, for his
house," [8] and that "no prayer is so truly or so properly mine,
as that that the Church hath delivered and recommended to

[4] *LXXX Sermons,* 76.
[5] *LXXX Sermons,* 9.
[6] *LXXX Sermons,* 13.
[7] *Ibid.*
[8] *LXXX Sermons,* 9.

me." [9] Donne held that as the law of the country was his, as the baptism and absolution given by the Church were his, so the prayers ordained by the Church were his too. He said, " You would scarce thanke a man for an extemporall Elegy, or Epigram or Panegyrique in your praise, if it cost the poet, or the orator no paines. God will scarce hearken to sudden inconsidered, irreverent prayers." He knew by his own personal experience how difficult it was for the soul and mind and intellect to attain in unison that serenity and calmness without which no sincere private prayer was possible.

He wrote, " When we consider with a religious seriousness the manifold weaknesses of the strongest devotions in time of Prayer, it is a sad consideration." [9] In an autobiographical passage he has described vividly the lack of concentration in private prayers.[10]

" I turn to hearty and earnest prayer to God, and I fix my thoughts strongly (as I thinke) upon him, and before I have perfected one petition, one period of my prayer, a power and principality is got in to me againe. . . . The spirit of slumber closes mine eyes, and I pray drowsily. . . . The spirit of deviation and vain repetition, and I pray giddily, and circularly, and returne againe and againe to that I have said before, and perceive not that I do so. . . . I pray not onely negligently, but erroniously, dangerously, for such things as disconduce to the glory of God, and my true happinesse, if they were granted. Nay, even the Prophet Hosea's *Spiritus fornicationum,* that is, some re-membrance of the wantonnesse of my youth, some mis-interpretation of a word in my prayer, that may bear an ill sense, some unclean spirit, some power or principality hath depraved my prayer, and slackened my zeale." [11]

It was to guard against this form of inconsiderate prayer in which the spirit of error and negligence enters and destroys the purpose and sincerity of private prayers that Donne

[9] *LXXX Sermons,* 80.
[10] Mr. Pearsall Smith has given in his anthology of Donne's sermons a passage on " Imperfect prayers " beginning—" I throw myselfe downe in my chamber . . . " which has been cited by many of Donne's critics as an example of his modern analytical habit of mind (Mr. Fausset says " And what a phenomenon is this of so modern and self conscious a mind moving in a world of mediæval thought "). There are several such passages in Donne's sermons as *LXXX Sermons,* 45, quoted above.
[11] *LXXX Sermons,* 45.

advised his congregation to cherish and value the liturgy and various prayers prescribed by the Church.

Donne, however, himself composed some beautiful prayers in his *Essays in Divinity,* and *Devotions upon Emergent Occasions,* and sometimes in his sermons we find prayers which he used to recite after his sermon to which he attached great importance. He said, " The Church is the house of prayer, so, as that upon occasion, preaching may be left out, but never a house of preaching, so as that prayer may be left out." [12]

We know from several references in his sermons that Donne realized the importance of prayer in the development of mystical consciousness.

" And it hath most wayes and addresses. . . . It may be vocall, for we may speake prayers. It may be actuall, for we do prayers—for deeds have voyce." [13]

He knew the beauty and serenity of mental prayer.

" I can build a church in my bosome, I can serve God in my heart, and never clouth my prayer in words. God is often said to *heare* and *answer* in the Scriptures, when they to whom he speaks, have said nothing." [14]

" When I pray in my chamber, I build a Temple there, that houre; And, that minute, when I cast out a prayer, in the street, I build a Temple there; And when my soule prays without any voyce, my very body is then a Temple." [15]

When God out of His loving kindness visits us even in our private devotions and blesses them, Donne asks is it proper that we should never go to the Church where He has promised to be always present.

" And shall not I come to his Temple where he is alwaies resident? My chamber were no Temple, my body were no Temple, except God came to it, but whether I came hither or no this will be God's temple : I may lose by my absence; he gains nothing by my coming." [15]

And though in prayer, whether we besiege God in the congregation or " wrestle with him hand to hand in our

[12] *LXXX Sermons,* 9.
[13] *L Sermons,* 34.
[14] *LXXX Sermons,* 26.
[15] *LXXX Sermons,* 4.

Chambers," [16] it is the only " way which God hath given us to batter Heaven." [16]

THE MYSTICAL LIFE

The division of the mystic way in three definite stages, Purgation, Illumination and Union, has been looked upon throughout the ages as merely diagrammatic, as loosely, answering to those mystical experiences which can never be classified so rigidly.

Even as early in the history of Christian mysticism as S. Augustine, we find him referring to seven degrees *(gradus)* in the operations of the soul, which is the principle of life, of sensation, of intelligence, of morality; the last three—which he calls *tranquillitas,* the calming of passions; *ingressio,* the approach to contemplation, the contemplation itself—correspond to Purgation, Illumination and Union. [17]

We shall try to describe Donne's conception of these mystical stages and briefly discuss how far he experienced them himself. No critic has approached Donne's mysticism from this point of view except Mrs. Simpson, who has referred to them in her discussion of " Donne's thought."

Conversion

Conversion, or the awakening of the self, precedes the stage of purgation. It is really the awakening of the transcendental consciousness. Donne attributes conversion to the Will of God in which the self is completely passive to the workings of Divine Grace.

> " Man in his conversion, is nothing, does nothing. His bodie is not verier dust in the grave, till a Resurrection, than his Soul is dust in his body, till a resuscitation by grace. But then this grace does not work upon this nothingness that is in man, upon this meere privation; but grace finds out mans naturall faculties, and exalts them to a capacity, and a susceptiblenesse of the working thereof, and so by the understanding infuses faith." [18]

Donne says that God follows in our conversion the same method which he adopted in our creation.

> " God proceeds in our Conversion, and regeneration, as

[16] *XXVI Sermons,* 22.
[17] *Western Mysticism,* by Dom Cuthbert Butler, p. 37.
[18] *LXXX Sermons,* p. 61.

he did in our first creation. There man was nothing; but God breathed not a soule into that nothing; but of a clod of earth he made a body, and into that body infused a soule."

Thus the Grace of God works on the natural faculties of man, creating in him an acute consciousness of his sin and of the need of repentance. The soul in conversion seems to have undergone a vitalizing experience in which new aspects of reality are revealed. Evelyn Underhill, speaking of this new consciousness, cites the example of S. Paul.

" In most cases, the onset of this new consciousness seems to the self so sudden, so clearly imposed from without rather than developed from within, as to have a supernatural character. The typical case is, of course, that of St. Paul: the sudden light, the voice, the ecstasy, the complete altera-tion of life." [19]

Donne has also referred to this experience of S. Paul in one of his sermons.

" The whole work of Almighty God, in the Conversion of man, is many times expressed by this act of shining; an effectual, a powerful shining: The light which shin'd upon S. Paul going to *Damascus,* struck him to the ground . . . and *S. Paul's* light was accompanied with a Voice." [20]

He has given a brief description of his own state of con-version in *Essays in Divinity,* in which his desire for working and thinking in complete harmony with the Divine Will is clearly expressed.

Donne, like the other mystics, also attributes his conversion to the " visitation " of God. It, too, seems to have been imposed from without rather than from within.

" Let this minute, O God, this happy minute of thy visitation, be the beginning of her (soul's) conversion, and shaking away confusion, darknesse, barrenesse, and let her now produce creatures, thoughts, words and deeds agreeable to thee."

The first effect of conversion, the awakening of the self, is the realization of the need of purification, of freedom from intellectual error and moral disorder.

The teaching on mystical theology of S. Bernard, who in the

[19] *Mysticism,* by Evelyn Underhill, p. 216.
[20] *XXVI Sermons,* 25.

opinion of Dean Inge[21] and Abbé P. Pourrat,[22] shaped the Catholic piety of the later Middle Ages and also of modern times, is contained in eighty-six sermons on the Canticle or " Song of Songs."[23]

Like S. Augustine and the other Christian mystics, S. Bernard thinks that in order to enjoy the bliss of " Contemplation," the soul must pass through the fire of purgation. Addressing his monks, S. Bernard emphasized the necessity of self-discipline, purification and mortification.

> " The taste for contemplation is not due except to obedience to God's Commandments. . . . ' What then would you have me to do ? ' ' In the first place I would have you cleanse your conscience from every defilement of anger and murmuring and envy and dispute. . . . In the next place I would wish you to adorn yourself with the flowers of good works and laudable studies of every kind, and seek the sweet perfumes of virtues . . . and endeavour to employ yourselves in them . . . that your conscience may everywhere be fragrant with the perfumes of piety, of peace, of gentleness, of justice, of obedience, of cheerfulness, of humility.' "[24]

To Donne the first sign of conversion is the consciousness of sin and the realization of the need of repentance and purification.

> " I acknowledged in myselfe, I came to a feeling in myselfe, what my sinfull condition was. This is our quickning in our regeneration, and second birth; and till this come, a sinner lies as the Chaos in the beginning of the Creation, before the *spirit of God had moved upon the face of the waters, Dark* and *voyd,* and *without forme.*"[25]

After this " sinful condition " has been realized, the need of repentance becomes an urgent necessity; and this process of purgation is a long and painful one. Julian of Norwich says,

---

[21] Dean Inge says, " His great achievement was to recall devout and loving contemplation to the image of the crucified Christ, and to found that Worship of our Saviour as the ' Bridegroom of the Soul ' which in the next centuries inspired so much fervid devotion and lyrical sacred poetry " (*Christian Mysticism,* p. 140).

[22] *Western Mysticism,* Chap. III.

[23] These were translated into English by S. J. Eales as *The Sermons on the Canticle* (1896).

[24] *Cant.* XLVI, 5, 7.

[25] *LXXX Sermons,* 58.

" I saw full surely that it behoveth needs to be that we should be in longing and in penance until the time that we be led so deep into God that we verily and truly know our own soul." [26]

To Donne also repentance is not a sudden remorse but a resurrection, the coming into life again of the soul after its sinful state, therefore it requires perseverance and is really a long and arduous task.

" Now every repentance is not a resurrection; It is rather a waking out of a dreame, than a rising to a new life. Nay it is rather a startling in our sleep, than any awaking at all, to have a sudden remorse, a sudden flash, and no constant perseverance. *Awake thou that sleepest,* says the Apostle, out of the Prophet: First *awake,* come to a sense of thy state; and then *arise from the dead,* says he, from the practise of dead works; and then *Christ shall give thee light;* life and strength to walk in new wayes. It is a long work and hath many steps. . . ." [27]

Donne says that true repentance consists in two things; it is a rejection of sin, and a final turning towards God.

" He that can not define Repentance, he that cannot spell it, may have it; and he that hath written whole books, great volumes of it, may be without it. In one word (one word will not do it, but in two words) it is *Aversio,* and *Conversio;* it is a turning from our sins, and a returning to our God." [28]

Donne, however, knew perhaps by his own personal experience that repentance and the realization of the horror of sin should begin early in life. Repentance in old age was of little importance in the sight of God.

" Wouldest thou consecrate a Chalice to God that is broken? No man would present a lame horse, a disordered clock, a torn book to the King . . . thy body is thy beast; and wilt thou present that to God, when it is lam'd and tir'd with excesse of wantonnesse? . . . Wilt thou then present thyself defac'd and mangled to Almighty God?" [29]

And as to the repentance on death-bed, he thought it was no

[26] *Revelations of Divine Love,* Cap. LVI.
[27] *LXXX Sermons,* 19.
[28] *XXVI Sermons,* 8.
[29] *XXVI Sermons,* 19.

repentance at all, for we are then not in the full control of our faculties and do not see our life in its true perspective.

" We do rather dream that we repent, then repent indeed, upon our death-bed. To him that travels by night a bush seems a tree, and a tree seems a man, and a man a spirit; nothing hath the true shape to him; to him that repents by night, on his death-bed, neither his own sins, nor the mercies of God have their true proportion." [30]

In the state of purgation and repentance the soul has a consciousness of its gradual shedding off the sin, and at the same time it implicitly relies on divine grace to preserve it from falling into sin again.

" So in this Soul, that hath this first Resurrection from sin, by grace, a conscience of her own infirmity, that she may relapse and yet a testimony of the powerfulnesse of God's spirit that easily she shall not relapse, may consist well together."

The first step according to Donne in the cleansing of the self is to receive sincerely the " helps," the Word and the Sacrament, which Christ has offered to the Soul in the Church.

" This *cleansing* then implies, that which we commonly call the enwrapping in the Covenant, the breeding in the visible Church . . . to live within the sound of his voyce, and within the reach of our spiritual food, the Word, and Sacraments. . . . This cleansing therefore, is that disposition, which God by his grace, infuses into us, That we stand in the congregation, and communion of Saints, capable of those mercies, which God hath by his Ordinance, annexed to these meetings." [31]

After receiving the full benefit of " God's grace exhibited in his ordinance " and after realizing that the " marks of his Grace are upon thee, that his spirit beares witness with thy spirit, that thy repentance hath been accepted by him," [32] the soul should strive to attain that purity of conscience without which the process of purgation can never be completed.

He says " A Conscience is not clean, by having recollected

[30] *Ibid.*
[31] *LXXX Sermons,* 64.
[32] *LXXX Sermons,* 54.

K

all her sinnes in the *Memory*," [33] for they may drive the soul
to desperation; the sins must be openly confessed, and thus
" emptied in the bottomlesse sea of the blood of Christ
Jesus," [34] and then we should be careful not even to have " a
sinfull delight in the Memory of those sins " which we have
already repented, for the aim of purification is the complete
emptying and stripping of the self, of all sinful and unreal
things which are harmful to the life of the soul.

Donne realizes that Purity and Holiness are indispensable
for the Illumination of the self.

" Purity, Sincerity, Integrity, Holinesse, is a skirt of
Christ's garment; It is the very livery that he puts upon us;
we cannot serve him without it (we must *serve him in
holiness, and purenesse*) we cannot see him without it, *without holinesse no man shall see God*. But then to be pure,
and not *peaceable,* to determine this purity in ourselves, and
condemne others, this is but an imaginary, but an illusory
purity." [35]

Eckhart has also said " God is pure Good in himself,
therefore will he dwell nowhere but in a pure soul. There he
can pour himself out: into that he can wholly flow." [36]

To Donne *Purification* is not a subjective state; it must be
expressed in humility, meekness and good works.

" How shall this purification appeare? It follows;
They shall be zealous of good works. They shall not
wrangle about faith and works, but be actually zealous of
good works . . . true purity is milde, meeke, humble, and to
despise and undervalue others is an inseparable mark of
false purity." [37]

According to Donne there are three dangers in purification
against which we must guard ourselves.

" There are three great dangers in this consideration of
perfectnesse, and purity; First to distrust of God's mercy,
if thou finde not this purity in thyselfe and this perfectnesse;
And then to presume upon God, nay upon thine owne right,
in an overvaluing of thine owne purity, and perfectnesse;

[33] *L Sermons*, 49.
[34] *Ibid.*
[35] *L Sermons*, 44.
[36] *Mysticism*, by Evelyn Underhill, p. 248.
[37] *LXXX Sermons*, 8.

And againe to condemne others whom thou wilt think lesse pure or perfect than thyselfe." [38]

S. Bernard held that the purification of the self should be accompanied by acts of piety.

" That good works are nourishment to the soul may be learned from the words : ' My meat is to do the will of him that sent me.' Therefore let works of piety accompany the labours of penitence which strengthen the soul " (Cant. XVIII, 5, 6).

Donne knew, like other mystics, that purity and love go hand in hand. He calls love " the noblest affection that the nature of man hath," [39] and defines it as " A holy impatience in being without it, or being in a jealousie that we are without it ; and it is a holy fervour and vehemency in the pursuit of it, and a preferring it before any other thing that can be compared to it : That's love." [39]

He explains how purity leads to the love of God.

" Therefore it deserves to be insisted upon . . . from the thing itself that is required (pureness) and the seat, and center of that pureness (the heart) and the way of this fixation of this pureness in the heart (detestation of former habits of sin and preventing of future sins, in a watchful consideration of all our actions, before we do them). We are come to that affection wherewith this inestimable pureness is to be embraced, love." [40]

Richard Rolle expressed the same truth when he said,

" Burning of love into a soul truly taken all vices purgeth . . . for whilst the true lover with strong and fervent desire into God is borne, all things him displease that from the sight of God withdraw." [41]

Too much has been written on Donne's acute sense of sin in general and his own sins of youth in particular to which he gave intense expression in his holy sonnets, devotions and sermons, but his passionate belief in the mercy of God, and efficacy of repentance and purgation is also evident in his sonnets as well as in his sermons.

[38] *LXXX Sermons*, 80.
[39] *XXVI Sermons*, 24.
[40] *Ibid.*
[41] Richard Rolle, *The Fire of Love*, Bk. I, Chap. XXIII.

> " Yet grace, if thou repent, thou canst no lacke;
> But who shall give thee that grace to beginne?
> Oh make thyself with holy mourning Blacke,
> And red with blushing, as thou art with Sinne;
> Or wash thee in Christ's blood, which hath this might
> That being red, it dyes red soules to white." [42]

Donne, in a remarkable passage in his sermons, says that though Christ has taken upon Himself the sins of all the world, every individual soul should bear the testimony of his remission in his own conscience, and this he calls the " sealing " of the Pardon.

> " In the knowledge that Christ hath taken all the sins of all the world upon himself, that there is enough done for the salvation of all mankinde, I have a shadowing, a refreshing; But because I can have no testimony, that this generall redemption belongs to me, who am still a sinner, except there passe some act between God and me, some investiture, some acquittance of my debts, my sins . . . and covers my sin, from the eye of his father, not onely *obumbrando,* as hee hath spread himselfe as a cloud refreshing the whole world, in the value of the satisfaction, but by coming to me, by spreading himself upon me, as the Prophet did upon the dead child, Mouth to mouth, Hand to hand." [43]

Donne knew that the knowledge of the self comes only through suffering and privation which God inflicts on the human soul.

> " So when the hand and sword of God hath pierced our soul, we are brought to a better knowledge of ourselves, than any degree of Prosperity would have raised us to." [44]

In another sermon Donne held that mortification was necessary to have an experience of Christ's " suffering in flesh."

> " There cannot be so great a crosse as to have none . . . for afflictions are our spiritual nourishment; I lacke one limb of that body I must grow into, which is the body of Christ Jesus, if I have no Crosses; for my conformity to Christ, (and that's my being made into his body) must be accomplished in my fulfilling his sufferings in his flesh." [45]

[42] *Holy Sonnets,* 9.
[43] *LXXX Sermons,* 56.
[44] *Ibid.*
[45] *L Sermons,* 17.

Mortification

Mortification has been called the positive aspect of purification; it consists in preserving chastity, which is the poverty of senses, and obedience, which is the poverty of the will, and the cultivation of these virtues results in the possession of divine love, which is the reward of purgation. Poverty is not the lack of things but the absence of the desire to possess anything; it is a state of complete detachment. S. John of the Cross said,

> " I am not speaking here of the absence of things, for absence is not detachment if the desire remains—but of that detachment which consists in suffering desire and avoiding pleasure. It is this that sets the soul free even though possession may be still retained." [46]

Donne thought that chastity should be practised early in life for " Chastity is not chastity in old man but a disability to be unchast; and therefore thou dost not give God that which thou pretendest to give, for thou hast no chastity to give him . . . but it is not . . . an old man comes to the infirmities of childhood again; but he comes not to the strength of youth again." [47]

Donne knew the weakness of human flesh and the frailty of human nature and realized the need of self-discipline and obedience; he pointed out that even Christ, in whom human nature reached its highest perfection, was not without human infirmity.

> " All other men, by occasion of this flesh, have darke *clouds,* yea *nights,* yea long and frozen winter nights of sinne, and of the *works of darknesse.* Christ was incapable of any such nights, or any such clouds, any approaches towards *sinne;* but yet Christ admitted some *shadows,* some such degrees of human infirmity . . . he was willing to show that the nature of man, in the best perfection thereof is not true light, all light . . . yet *Father,* whatsoever the sadness of my soule have made mee say, *yet, not my will but thine be done; not mine, but thine;* So that they were not altogether *all one;* humane infirmity made some difference. So that no man, not Christ, considered but so as man was *tota lux,* all light, no cloud." [48]

[46] Quoted by Evelyn Underhill, *Mysticism*, p. 235.
[47] *XXVI Sermons,* 19.   [48] *L Sermons,* 36.

But Donne was against the extreme forms of mortification, which he called "those devilish doctrines (so S. Paul calls them)" [49] which forbid certain meats and "make uncommanded macerations of the body, without eating anything at all." [49] He said that as man consists of both soul and body, he should "by a sober and temperate life make his body obsequious, and serviceable to his soule, but yet leave his soule a body to worke in and an organ to praise God upon, both in a devout humiliation of his body, in God's service, and in a bodily performance of the duties of some calling." [49]

He declared that "neither spirit nor flesh must be destroyed in us; a spirituall man is not all spirit, he is a man still." [50] Donne was vehemently against the monkish form of asceticism.

"Wee must not thinke to depart from the offices of society, and duties of a calling, and hide ourselves in Monasteries, or in retired lives, for fear of tentations; but when a tentation attempts us, to come with that authority and that powerfull exorcisme of Nazianzen. . . . Depart from me, lest the Cross of Christ, in my hand, overthrow you. For a sober life, and a Christian mortification, and discreet discipline, are crosses derived from the Crosse of Christ Jesus, and animated by it, and it may be alwaies in a readiness to crosse such tentations." [51]

Illumination

Donne claimed for himself nothing but the guidance afforded to the Christian soul in the Word, Sacrament and the Ordinances of the Church.

"That the best means of knowing Christ is in his Church. . . . I know nothing, if I know not Christ crucified, And I know not that, if I know not how to apply him to myselfe, nor doe I know that, if I embrace him not in those meanes which he hath afforded me in his Church, in his Word, and Sacraments. If I neglect this meanes, this place, these exercises, howsoever I may satisfie myselfe, with an overvaluing mine own knowledge at home, I am so far from fulnesse, as that vanity itself is not more empty." [52]

[49] *LXXX Sermons*, 21.
[50] *LXXX Sermons*, 1.
[51] *LXXX Sermons*, 55.
[52] *LXXX Sermons*, 79.

He thought that though God had revealed Himself in the doctrine and sacraments of the Church, in order to recognize Him in His Church, our spirit should bear witness to His spirit in our souls.   He compares the Church to God's Face and His Spirit working in the Christian soul to the Eye of God.

" God's whole ordinance in his Church, is God's face; For that is the face of God, by which God is manifested to us; But then, that eye in that face, by which he promises to guide us . . . is that blessed Spirit of his, by whose opera- tion he makes that grace, which does evermore accompany his ordinance, effectual upon us; The whole congregation sees God face to face, in the Service, in the Sermon, in the Sacrament, but there is an eye in that face . . . a piercing and operating spirit that looks upon that soul and foments and cherishes that soul, who by a good use of God's former grace, is become fitter for his present." [53]

We find a note of ecstatic joy in Donne's contemplation of the Love and Beauty of God.

" O glorious beauty, infinitely reverend, infinitely fresh and young, we come late to thy love, if we consider the past daies of our lives, but early if thou beest pleased to reckon with us from this house of the shining of thy grace upon us." [54]

These words remind us of S. Augustine's great rhapsody about the love of God.

" Too late loved I thee, O Beauty so old, yet ever new : to late loved I thee.   And behold thou wert within and I abroad and there I searched for thee. . . . Thou breathedst odours, and I drew in breath, and pant for thee.   I tasted, and hunger and thirst.   Thou touchedst me, and I was on fire for thy peace." [55]

Evelyn Underhill has pointed out that " a joyous apprehension of the Absolute," [56] and " a pleasure-state of the intensest kind " [57] are the common characteristics of Illumination. Illumination also meant to Donne an ever-increasing sancti- fication of life resulting in a " holy cheerfulness," which he

[53] *LXXX Sermons,* p. 617.
[54] *XXVI Sermons,* 18.
[55] *Western Mysticism,* pp. 40–1.
[56] *Mysticism,* p. 288.
[57] *Ibid.,* p. 290.

considers to be the best evidence of the possession of heavenly
life on earth.

" In a true Church there are many outward badges and
marks, by which others may judge, and pronounce mee to
bee a true Christian ; But . . . the inward badge and marke,
by which I know this in myself, is joy ; The blessednesse of
heaven itselfe, salvation and the fruits of Paradise, (that
Paradise which cannot be expressed, cannot be comprehended) have yet got no other name in the subtilty of the
Schools, nor in the fulnesse of the Scriptures, but to be
called the Joys of Heaven. . . ." [58]
Donne says that the true mark of the illumined mystic is the
possession of this joy.

" Certainly as that man shall never see the Father of
Lights after this, to whom the day never breaks in this life :
As that man must never look to walk with the Lamb wheresoever he goes in heaven, that ranne away from the Lamb
whensoever he came towards him, in this life ; so he shall
never possess the joys of heaven hereafter, that feels no joy
here." [58]
He declared that " true joy in this world shall flow into the
joy of Heaven, as a River flowes in to the sea."   This joy will
not be finished at death, and another infused in Heaven, but
the latter shall be a continuation and multiplication of the joy
that the soul possessed in its earthly life, for Christ says of the
heavenly joys " our joy might be full," that is, " perfected,
sealed with an everlastingnesse."   Donne calls this joy an
" inward blessing " [59] and the " seales " [59] of God's favour.

This idea of interior joy and sweetness is also characteristic
of S. Augustine's description of his own illumination.
S. Augustine says that the soul in " contemplation experiences
such joys, such a full enjoyment of the highest and truest Good,
such a breath of serenity and eternity, as are indescribable."
S. Augustine also believed that the joys felt by the soul in the
mystical experience was a foretaste of the heavenly joys.
Describing the joy of his own mystical experience, S. Augustine

[58] *L Sermons,* 16.
[59] Comparing the joys of youth to this holy joy of the Illumined Soul,
Donne beautifully says :   "And as the Sunne may say to the Starres at
Noone, How frivolous and impertinent a thing is your light now?   So
this joy shall say *unto laughter* (of youth) *Thou are mad,* and *unto
mirth, what dost thou? "* (*LXXX Sermons,* 79).

declared : Were this prolonged, and the vision ravish and
absorb and wrap up its beholder in inward joys, so that life
might be for ever like that one moment of understanding;
were not this the entry in to the joy of Heaven ?[60]

Donne says that the blessedness of the Purified and the
Illumined Soul is not a comparative blessedness, but actual
and absolute.

" The pure in heart are blessed already, not onely com-
paratively, that they are in a better way of Blessednesse,
than others are, but actually in a present possession of it :
for this world and the next world, are not, to the pure in
heart, two houses, but two roomes, a Gallery to passe
through, and a Lodging to rest in, in the same House, which
are both under one roofe, Christ Jesus . . . so the joy, and
the sense of Salvation, which the pure in heart have here,
is not a joy severed from the Joy of Heaven, but a joy that
begins in us here, and continues, and accompanies us
thither, and there flowes on, and dilates itselfe to an infinite
expansion." [61]

DONNE AND CHRIST

A passionate devotion to the Person of Christ, as the
Saviour, Redeemer and Lover is the keynote of Donne's
mysticism.   Donne held that we could have no foretaste of
the joy of Heaven in this life without the birth of Christ in
our soul.

" In this fulnesse, in this coming of our Saviour into us,
. . . we should finde a threefold fullnesse in ourselves ; we
should find a fulness of grace, a daily sense of improvement,
growth in grace, a filling of all former vacuities, a supplying
of all emptiness in our soules, till we come to Stephens
fullnesse, Full of the holy Ghost and wisdome, and full of
the holy Ghost and Faith, and full of faith and power ; And
so we should come to finde a fulnesse of glory, that is in an
apprehension and inchoation of heaven in this life." [62]

[60] Conf., IX, 25.
[61] LXXX Sermons, 12.
[62] LXXX Sermons, 3. As against this threefold birth of Christ in the
human soul, there have been three " advents " of Christ. " An Advent
of Humiliation, when he came in flesh, an Advent of glory, when he
shall come to judgement, and between these an advent of grace, which
is the Advent of the Holy Ghost when Christ works in us, the Holy
Ghost comes to us " (LXXX Sermons, 36).

Donne, like all other Christian mystics, maintained that there were two aspects of the relation of the soul to Christ; the birth of Christ in the soul, which makes us " a new creature in Christ Jesus," [63] and a " dying " in Christ. He has described the psychological change which happens in the man who dies in Christ.

" Now of this dying Man, that dies in Christ . . . must we give you a Picture too. . . . His understanding and his will is all one faculty. He understands God's purpose upon him, and he would not have God's purpose turned any other way'; he sees God will dissolve him, and he would faine be dissolved, to be with Christ; His understanding and his will is all one faculty; His memory and his fore-sight are fixt, and concentrated upon one object, upon goodnesse." [64]

Donne has several times employed the imagery and symbolism of human love to express Christ's love for the individual soul. Following the orthodox tradition of Christian mysticism, he has also used this erotic symbolism in its other meaning [65] when Christ is the Bridegroom and the Church is the Bride. Donne, speaking of the " widowhood " of the Bride (the Church) soon after Christ's Ascension says,

" When that Church that mourned, and lamented his absence, when she was but his *spouse*, must necessarily mourn now in a more vehement manner, when she was to be (in some sense) his widow; when that *shepherd* was not only to be *smitten*, and so the *flock dispersed* (this was done in his passion) but he was to be taken away, in his Ascension." [66]

When Donne depicts Christ as the Bridegroom and the individual soul as the Bride, it is not Christ in His Humanity that is married to the soul but Christ as Logos. Donne, speaking of the marriage of the soul with Christ, declared,

" And of this second, the spiritual marriage much needs not to be said; There is another priest that contracts that, another Preacher that celebrates it, the spirit of God to our spirit . . . there is a marriage and Christ marries me. . . . And he hath married it in *æternum*, for ever; . . . but this eternity is not begun in this world, but from all eternity in

[63] *XXVI Sermons*, 16.   [65] *LXXX Sermons*, 26.
[64] *XXVI Sermons*, 15.   [66] *LXXX Sermons*, 36.

Book of Life in God's eternall Decree for my election, there Christ was married to my soul." [67]

S. Bernard, in his classical *Sermons on the Canticle,* has clearly expressed the meaning and significance of his use of the symbolism of human love to denote the spiritual and mystical " states " of the soul.

" Take heed that you bring chaste ears to this discourse of love; and when you think of these two lovers, remember always that not a man and a women are to be thought of, but the Word of God and a Soul. And if I shall speak of Christ and the Church, the sense is the same except that under the name of the Church is specified not one soul only, but the united souls of many, or rather their unanimity " (Cant. LXI, 2).

In his sermon on Psalms ii—xii, Donne makes *Kiss* the symbol of the love of Christ.

" No man comes to God, except the Father draw him; the Father draws no man, but by the Son, and that Son receives none but by love, and this cement and glue, of a zealous and reverentiall love, a holy kisse. Kisse the Son. . . ." [68]

Defending his use of this " love-imagery " Donne declared,

" But though this act of love, be so defamed both wayes, by treachery, by licentiousness, yet God chooses this Metaphore, he bids us kisse the Sonne. It is true, and an usefull Rule that . . . May things not ill in themselves, though deflected and dietorted to ill, be restored to good againe; and therefore doth God, in more than this one place expect our love in a kisse; for if we be truly in love with him, it will be a holy and an acceptable Metaphore unto us, else it will have a carnall and a fastidious taste." [68]

Explaining the spiritual nature of the " Mystic kiss " S. Bernard says,

" The kiss of his Mouth signifies nothing else than to receive the inpouring of the Holy Spirit. . . . The Bride has the boldness to ask trustingly that the inpouring of the Holy Spirit may be granted to her under the name of a kiss " (Cant. VIII, 2–6).

The mystics believe that the state of the joyful communion

[67] *L Sermons,* 3.
[68] *LXXX Sermons,* 41.

with God is often interrupted by a period of intense spiritual isolation in which God seems to desert the soul. In the Dark Night of the Soul or " the Absence of God," the active sense of sin, the consciousness that God has deserted the soul, and the agony of spiritual desolation which the soul experiences are really the means by which the soul is finally purged and purified so that it might be ready for the " unitive life."

S. John of the Cross has described with an acute psychological insight the state of the Soul in the Dark Night.

" The afflictions and distress of the Will now are also very great; they occasionally pierce the Soul with a sudden recollection of the evils that environ it, and of the Uncertainty of relief. To this is superadded the memory of Past happiness; for they who enter this night have generally, had much sweetness in God, and served him greatly; but now, to see themselves strangers to so much happiness, and unable to recover it, causes them the great affliction." [69]

S. John of the Cross says that the cause of this spiritual affliction is that " when the rays of this pure light shine upon the soul, in order to expel its impurities, the soul perceives itself to be so unclean and miserable that it seems as if God had set himself against it, and itself were set against God." [70] According to S. John the Soul in the Dark Night undergoes the Purgation of the Spirit, while the Purgation before Illumination is really the purification of the senses.

Donne has several times alluded to the Dark Night of the Soul in his sermons.

" Love him not onely in spiritual transfigurations when he visits thy soule with glorious consolations, but even in his inward eclipses, when he withholds his comforts, and withdraws his cheerfulnesse, even when he makes as though he knew not thee, Love him." [71]

Union

The main distinction between Illumination and Union is that in illumination the mystic in spite of his heightened spiritual consciousness, retains the individuality of his self intact and separate from God; while in the unitive life, the

[69] *The Dark Night of the Soul*, trans. by David Lewis, p. 88.
[70] *The Dark Night of the Soul*, p. 31.
[71] *LXXX Sermons*, 70.

" union with God has now been finally established," [72] and that the self of the mystic, though intact, has been wholly permeated with God. It is in the union of the soul with God in which, says S. Bernard, we should not imagine anything physical.

> " But be most careful not to allow yourself to think that we perceive anything corporeal or by way of images in this Union of the Word with the Soul. I am saying only that which the Apostle says, that ' he that joined to God is one spirit.' The Union *(conjunctio)* then, is made in the spirit, because God is a Spirit."

Speaking of the necessity of this inward union of the soul with the Bridegroom, S. Bernard says,

> " She (the Soul) desires that he whom she loves should not show himself to her in an outward shape, but should be, as it were, inpoured into her; that he should not merely appear to her, but should enter into and possess her; nor is it doubtful that her happiness is so much the greater, as he is within rather than without " (Cant. XXXI, 4–6).

We do not know whether Donne himself reached the unitive stage of mystical life or not, but he once declared, " I will finde out another death, *mortem raptus,* a death of rapture and of extasie, that death which S. Paul died more than once." We can never know whether he experienced this death of ecstasy which he describes as " a kinde of buriall and sepulchre, and rest of the soule." [73] But in one of his sermons while describing the nature of the soul's union with God, he speaks as if he believed that he had attained union with Christ in this life.

> " My Soule is united to my Saviour, now in my life, as in death, and I am already made one *spirit with him;* and whatsoever death can doe, this kisse, this union, can doe, that is, give me a present, an immediate possession of the Kingdome of Heaven." [74]

In another sermon Donne, using the symbolism of the " Song of Songs," declared that Christ was married to his soul.

> " And as he hath married me to him, in *æternum,* for

[72] E. Underhill, *Mysticism,* p. 499.
[73] *LXXX Sermons,* 27.
[74] *LXXX Sermons,* 41.

ever, before all beginnings, and in *æternum,* for ever, without any interruptions, so I know that *whom he loves he loves to the end,* and that he hath given me, not a presumptuous impossibility but a modest infallibility, that no sin of mine shall divorce or separate me from him." [75]

But Donne makes a clear distinction between a momentary vision of God in the life, and the vision of God as He is, in His Essence, which is reserved for the soul in Heaven, and which no man can see in this life.

"Here we may be in his Presence, we see his *State;* there we are in his Bedchamber, and see his eternall and glorious Rest." [76]

This is the orthodox view of the Christian mystics. S. Bernard also believed that God in His Essence cannot be seen in this life.

"God now appears as he wishes, not as he is. No wise man, no saint, no prophet, is able to see him as he is, nor has been able in this mortal body" (Cant. XXXI, 2).

Though S. Augustine held that Moses and S. Paul both saw God "face to face," it was the vision which was rarely granted to the mystics in this life.

"In this life contemplation is rather in faith, and with a very few through a mirror in enigma, and in part, in some vision of unchangeable Truth." [77]

Donne says that the end of our salvation is the union with God.

"That which is our end, Salvation, we call it *visionem Dei,* the sight of God, and we call it *unionem,* an Union with God: we shall *see* God, and we shall be united to God: for our seeing, we shall see him . . . as he is." [78]

God is blessedness, and our blessedness consists in our union with Him, "Our blessednesse is our possession; our union with God," [79] but this blessedness cannot be attained without Purity.

"The Substance of the Blessednesse is in this that I shall see God; *Blessed are the pure in heart,* sayes Christ, for

[75] *L Sermons,* 3.
[76] *L Sermons,* 10.
[77] *Western Mysticism,* p. 88.
[78] *L Sermons.*
[79] *Ibid.,* 44.

they shall see God.   If they should not see God, they were
not blessed." [80]
But absolute Purity cannot be attained in this life.

"Absolute pureness can not be attained *In via,* It is
reserved for us *In Patria;* At home in heaven, not in our
journey here, is that pureness to be expected.   But here in
the way, there is a degree of it acceptable to God." [81]
And though the vision of God as He is, is reserved for Heaven,
we can nevertheless have a momentary vision of God here.

"Though then the consummation of this Blessednesse
be that *visio Dei,* that sight of God, which in our glorified
state we shall have in heaven, yet, . . . there is an
inchoation thereof in this world." [82]
But the highest degree of knowledge and blessedness is
reserved for the soul in Heaven.

"There in heaven, I shall have *Continuitatem Intuendi;*
It is not only *vision,* but *intuition,* not only seeing, but a
beholding, a contemplating of God, and that in *continuitate,*
I shall have an uninterrupted, an un-intermitted, an un-
discontinued sight of God; I shall looke, and never look
off; not looke againe, as here, but looke, and looke still
. . . here I never saw myself, but in disguises; There, then,
I shall see myself, and see God too. . . . There I shall see
God intirely, all God . . . I myself shall be all light to see
that light by . . . there I shall be all light, no shadow upon
me; my soule invested in the light of joy and my body
in the light of glory." [83]

[80] *LXXX Sermons,* 17.
[81] *LXXX Sermons.*
[82] *LXXX Sermons,* 56.
[83] *L Sermons,* 44.

APPENDIX TO CHAPTER II

JOHN DONNE ON CONVERSION [1]

DONNE in a letter to Sir Robert Ker (April, 1627) said :
"My tenents are always for the preservation of the religion I was born in, and the peace of the state, and the rectifying of the conscience."

E. Gosse, commenting on this letter, said :
"The words here, 'the religion I was born in,' are very startling, and at first sight incomprehensible. Everybody knew that Donne had been born and bred a Romanist, and that his family were stringent recusants. . . . But I think that Donne, as a staunch High Churchman, would not admit any essential difference between the Catholic religion, in which he was born, and that which he now professed. . . . If, as Dr. James Gairdner has said, 'Rome was no longer competent to be the guardian either of faith or morals,' the Catholic religion in England, as in Italy, was none the less one and indivisible." [2]

These remarks of E. Gosse give the impression that it was the only place where Donne had expressed himself on this subject. While recently preparing an anthology of Donne's sermons, illustrative of his theology and mysticism, I came across several passages where he has definitely declared himself against changing one's religion, and fully explained the meaning and significance of his conception of the Catholic Church.

In one of his sermons Donne declared :
"Truly I have been sorry to see some persons converted from the Roman Church to ours; because I have known, that onely *temporall respects* have moved them, and they have lived after rather in nullity or *indifference to either* religion, than in a true and established zeale."

And he went on to tell the story of a "French gentleman"
"who was turned from the Reformed to the Roman religion being asked, halfe in jest : 'Sir, which is the best

[1] Reproduced from *Theology*, April 1936.
[2] *The Life and Letters of John Donne*, by E. Gosse, Vol. II, p. 247.

religion, you must needs know, that have been of both?'
'Certainly, the religion I left, the *reformed religion* must
needs be the best religion, for when I changed, I had this
religion, the *Romans' religion,* for it, and three hundred
crowns a year to boot,' which was a pension given him upon
his conversion." [3]

In a letter to Sir Henry Goodyer (1613), Donne declared
that the " sound true opinion, that in all Christian professions
there is way to Salvation," should not make us indifferent or
weak in our own religion; and he compared the minds of the
people who have changed their religion to the ugliness of the
coins which have received more than one impression. He
said, " You shall seldom see a coin, upon which the stamp
were removed, though to imprint it better, but it looks awry
and squint. And so, for the most part, do minds which have
received divers impressions." [4]

Donne believed that conversion from one form of faith
to the other was only justified if there was any error in
fundamental doctrines. He said :

" Let none divorce himself from that religion, and that
worship of God, which God put into his armes, and which
he embraced in his Baptism. Except there be errour in
fundamental points, such as make that Church no Church,
let no man depart from that Church and that religion in
which he delivered himself to the service of God at first." [5]
He believed that we should deliver our religion in its totality
to posterity, for then alone it can be an inheritance.

Donne thought that all things which were necessary for
salvation were taught in the Anglican Church, and therefore
there was no need to know and imitate the " forms " of the
foreign Churches. He said :

" Trouble not thyselfe to know the formes and fashions
of forraine particular Churches; neither of a Church in the
Lake, nor a Church upon seven hills; but since God hath
planted thee in a Church, where all things necessary for
Salvation are administered to thee, and where no erronious

[3] *L Sermons,* 25.
[4] *The Life and Letters of John Donne,* by E. Gosse, Vol. II, p. 78.
[5] *L Sermons.* Donne had declared in his III Satire that one could
only believe in and follow one religion :
" . . . but unmoved thou
of force must one, and forc'd but one allow."

doctrine (even in the Confession of our Adversaries) is affirmed and held, that is the hill, and that is the Catholique Church, and there is this Commission in this text, meanes of Salvation sincerely executed." [6]

Donne held that the Anglican Church was the true Apostolic and Catholic Church, for it taught the same religion

"that Christ Jesus and his Apostles proposed at beginning, the same that the generall Councels established after, the same that the blessed Fathers of those times, unanimesly, and dogmatically delivered, the same that those glorious Martyrs quickened by their death, and carryed over all the world in the rivers, in the seas of their blood . . ." [7]

Donne defined the Catholic Church as the Church "wherein she is harmonious, that is those universal and fundamental doctrines which in all Christian Churches have been agreed by all to be necessary to Salvation"; and addressing his audience he declared:

"Then thou are a true Catholique. Otherwise, that is, without relation to this Catholique and universall doctrine to call a particular Church Catholique (that is, universall in dominion, but not in doctrine) in such a solecisme, as to speak of a white blackness or a great littlenesse; a particular Church to be universall, implies such a Contradiction." [8]

Donne did not believe, as Gosse seems to suggest, that the Anglican and the Roman Catholic Churches were identical. There were certain things in which he thought that the Anglican Church should not conform to the Roman Catholic Church. Donne in a letter to Sir Robert Ker (1624), while comparing the Spanish and Anglican Churches, said:

"But the difference of our situation is in North and South. . . . There are things in which we may, and in that wherein we should not, my hope is in God and in him,

---

[6] *LXXX Sermons,* 76; also see *L Sermons,* 33.

[7] *L Sermons,* 18.

[8] Donne had defined the Catholic Church in a similar way in *Pseudo-Martyr* (1610), but this definition has escaped the notice of his critics.

"That therefore is *Catholique* faith, which hath beene alwaies and everywhere taught; and *Repentance* and *Remission* of sinnes by the *Death* and *Resurrection of Christ,* and such truthes as the *Gospell* teaches, are that *Doctrine* which Coagulates and gathers the Church in to a body, and makes it Catholique" (*Pseudo-Martyr,* p. 373).

in whom God hath so evidently work, we shall not meet. Amen." [9]

It was in its preservation of the continuity of the Holy [10] Orders, in its following the ancient creeds,[11] in its preaching the fundamental doctrines common to all the Christian Churches, that Donne, like Bishop Andrewes and Laud,[12] held the Anglican Church to be the true Catholic Church.

[9] Donne had a shrewd idea of the difference between the French and Spanish Churches. Describing the character of Servin, he remarked: "He is a Catholic, but a French Catholic, and Sir, French papistry is but like French velvet—a pretty slack Religion, that would sooner wear out, and not of the three-piled papistry of Italy and Spain" (Gosse, Vol. I, p. 288).

[10] *L Sermons*, 40. In this sermon he maintained that the Anglican Church, like the Roman Church, had an "orderly derivation of power from one to another."

[11] In *L Sermons*, 14, Donne said that the Anglican Church enjoins that "the three Creeds (that of the Councell of Nice, that of Athanasius, and that which is commonly known by the name of the Apostles creed) ought thoroughly to be received and embraced."

[12] Laud had declared in his conference with Fisher, the Jesuit, that he could never allow the Roman Church its claim to be the only true Catholic Church. He said: "For 'the Church' may import in our language 'the only true Church' and perhaps, as some of you may seem to make it, 'the root and the ground of the Catholic.' And this I never did grant of the Roman Church, nor even mean to do. But 'a Church' can imply no more than that it is a member of the whole. And this I never did nor ever will deny, if it fall not absolutely away from Christ" (*A Relation of the Conference between William Laud and Mr. Fisher the Jesuit*, edited by C. H. Simpkinson, 1901).

BIBLIOGRAPHY

THE Bibliography is not intended to be exhaustive. All the books which have been consulted in the preparation of the thesis have not been included.

WORKS

1. A. B. GROSART, *Complete Poems*, 2 vols., Fuller Worthies' Library, *1872–3*.
2. J. R. and C. E. NORTON, *Poems from the Text of the Editions of 1633*, New York, 1895.
3. E. K. CHAMBERS, *Poems with an Introduction by George Saintsbury*, 2 vols., 1896.
4. C. E. NORTON, *Love Poems*, Boston, 1923.
5. H. J. C. GRIERSON, *The Poems of John Donne*, 2 vols., 1912.
6. J. HAYWARD, *Complete Poetry and Selected Prose*, 1929.
7. H. ALFORD, *Collected Works of John Donne*, with a Memoir, 6 vols., 1839.
8. A. JESSOPP, *Essays in Divinity*, 1855.
9. L. P. SMITH, *Donne's Sermons: Selected Passages with an Essay*, 1920.
10. J. SPARROW, *Devotions upon Emergent Occasions*, 1923.
11. J. KEYNES, *Ten Sermons*, 1923.

CRITICISM

12. E. GOSSE, *The Life and Letters of John Donne*, 2 vols., 1899.
13. H. J. C. GRIERSON, *The First Half of the Seventeenth Century; The Cross-Currents in the Seventeenth Century Literature; The Cambridge History of English Literature*, Vol. IV, Chapter XI. *The Metaphysical Lyrics and Poems of the Seventeenth Century.*
14. A. JESSOPP, *John Donne*, 1897.
15. H. I'A. FAUSSET, *Donne, A Study in Discord*, 1924.
16. P. LEGOUIS, *Donne the Craftsman*, 1927.
17. M. F. MILTON, *The Rhetoric of John Donne's Verse*, 1906.
18. E. SIMPSON, *A Study of the Prose Works of John Donne*, 1924. *A Chronological Arrangement of Donne's Sermons*, Modern Review VIII, 1913.
19. RUPERT BROOKE, *John Donne, Poetry and Drama*, 1913.
20. SAMUEL JOHNSON, *Lives of the Poets*, 1779.
21. BEN JOHNSON, *Conversation with Drummond of Hawthornden.*
22. JOHN DRYDEN, *Essay on Satire*, 1693.
23. S. T. COLERIDGE, *Notes and Lectures upon Shakespeare and some of the older Poets and Dramatists; Notes on English Divines.*
24. IZAAK WALTON, *Lives.*
25. LESLIE STEPHEN, "John Donne," *National Review*, XXIV, 595.
26. ARTHUR SYMONS, "John Donne," *The Fortnightly Review*, Series LXVI, 734.
27. E. GOSSE, *Seventeenth Century Studies*, 1883. *Jacobean Poets*, 1884.

28. G. WILLIAMSON, *The Donne Tradition*, 1930.
29. THEODORE SPENCER, *A Garland for John Donne*, 1931.
30. JOHN SPARROW, "Donne's Religious Development," *Theology*, March, 1931. *John Donne and Contemporary Preachers; Essays and Studies, English Association*, Vol. XVI.
31. L. I. BREVOLD, *The Religious Thought of Donne in Relation to Mediæval and Later Traditions; The Naturalism of Donne in Relation to some Renaissance Traditions. Jor. of Eng. and Ger. Phil.*, 1923.
32. G. N. CLARK, *The Seventeenth Century.*
33. E. DOWDEN, *New Studies in Literature*, 1845.
34. ARTHUR SYMONS, *The Figures of Several Centuries*, 1916.
35. ROBERT SENCOURT, *Outflying Philosophy.*
36. W. H. HUTTON, "John Donne, Poet and Preacher," *Theology*, Vol. IX, 1924.
37. J. A. SHAPIRO, *Text of Donne's Letters. Rev. of English Studies*, Vol. VII, 1931.
38. H. READ, *Reason and Romanticism*, 1927. *Phases of English Poetry.*
39. C. SPURGEON, *Mysticism in English Literature*, 1913.
40. H. C. BEECHING, *Religio Laici.*
41. G. TEGGARD, *Circumference Varieties of Metaphysical Verse*, 1929.
42. E. WENDELL, *The Temper of the Seventeenth Century in English Literature.*
43. BASIL WILBY, *The Seventeenth Century Background*, 1934.
44. J. B. LEISHMAN, *The Metaphysical Poets: Donne, Herbert, Vaughan, Traherne*, 1934.
45. J. BENNETT, *Four Metaphysical Poets*, 1934.